LETTERS FROM AN ENGLISH VIL

Cover: View of Nadderbourne from a painting by Roger Pearce

Ralph Whitlock

LETTERS FROM AN ENGLISH VILLAGE

Ralph Whitlock

A Selection of Articles from
The Guardian Weekly *1979-1987*

Illustrations by Roger Pearce

EX LIBRIS PRESS

First published in 1988 by
Ex Libris Press
1 The Shambles
Bradford on Avon
Wiltshire

Cover by 46 Design, Bradford on Avon
Typeset in 11 on 13 Plantin by
Saxon Printing Ltd., Derby
Printed in Great Britain by A Wheaton & Co. Ltd., Exeter

ISBN 0 948578 15 7

CONTENTS

FOREWORD

When we first met, I was staying in a cottage on the Sudeley Castle estate in Gloucestershire and Ralph Whitlock was in the cottage next door. It was a happy accident, for as a result he began contributing articles to *The Guardian Weekly* – this book is a selection from them. (He also taught me how to dowse for water, a skill I have not so far been able to put to much practical use; in my part of England the problem most summers is getting rid of the water, not finding it.)

People buy newspapers for different reasons and with different priorities, but from the correspondence that pours into our office from all parts of the world it is clear that few readers miss the Whitlock column. There may be scandals in Washington (there usually are), divisions in the leadership of the Soviet Communist Party, hijackings and hostage-taking in the Middle East, English football hooligans on the rampage through every capital of Europe, a falling (or rising) pound, a rising (or falling) dollar – but in Ralph Whitlock there is an island of sanity and Wiltshire common sense.

John Perkin
Editor
The Guardian Weekly

INTRODUCTION

The village is Nadderbourne, a name which you will not find on any map. Not that that matters, for it could be any one of the nine thousand or so villages that are the knots which fasten together the fabric of the English countryside.

In one of them I was born and reared; in another I am enjoying my evening years. Most of the intervening decades have found me deeply immersed in the humble affairs of farm and field, of lane and hedgerow. It is true that I have made eventful sorties to fashion another career in radio and television (middle-aged readers may remember *Cowleaze Farm*) and in journalism, and in five years' service with a mission charity I was able to savour something of other people's countrysides. But always I have been drawn back like a summer swallow to the thatched barns, the puddled tracks, the placid cows, the smooth turf of billowing downs, and the comfortable companionship of amiable neighbours that for me are home.

So when the editor of *The Guardian Weekly* invited me to write a weekly letter from my English village I accepted with alacrity. *The Guardian Weekly* has, in addition to a sound home base, an international readership which includes many expatriates, and my letters have tended to develop into a two-way correspondence. Readers write to me from Bolivia and Bhutan, from Papua and Pekin, from Wellington in New Zealand and Wellington in Somerset, and the general tone of their letters is nostalgic.

'I am writing to let you know how much I appreciate your articles in The Guardian Weekly. *I use your first name because I feel I know you as an old friend...' (Papua New Guinea)*

'Your charming style makes your profound philosophy very effective.' (Tanzania)

'Although I am not English, your letters invoke a feeling of nostalgia.' (Japan)

'Ralph tells us the things we want to know about the English countryside. Long may we have the privilege of being among his most ardent fans.' (Australia)

'I am a great fan of your column and, doubtless like thousands of others, revel in your encyclopaedic knowledge of English country life.' (Dubai)

I was fortunate in being born to middle-aged parents! My father was a small farmer – he would now be called a peasant farmer – who had begun his working life (at the age of twelve) as a shepherd boy. Conversation at our table when I was a boy tended to be about times past, about the unlikely attitudes and escapades of people who were, to me, staid and elderly. I absorbed much information about obsolete or dying customs and beliefs. I think I was as much at home in the Edwardian or even the Victorian countryside as that of the 1920s.

That is perhaps why I take such a pleasure in the conversations I have from time with my long-deceased great-grandfather William, and, occasionally, with great-grandmother Elizabeth, whom I meet down the orchard under the old apple-tree where his cider-press used to stand. Although more than a hundred years separate his time from ours, his observations on the current scene are far from being irrelevant. His allegory on Pop-Gun Percy, made at the time of the American bombing of Libya, could hardly be more apposite.

From very near the beginning of my letters readers have been demanding a collection of them in book form, and now, at last, I am managing to respond.

I often think, when I am composing these weekly letters, of my illustrious predecessors – Gilbert White, writing from Selborne, Richard Jefferies at Coate, W H Hudson, who haunts around Winterbourne Bishop (Martin). I know well, the tragic genius John Clare. Clare lamented the passing of the England of open fields, then dissolving before his eyes; Hudson witnessed the final chapter of the golden age of downland sheep; Jefferies was aware of the amoeba of Swindon reaching out to engulf his beloved countryside. And I too am a chronicler of a passing age. Indeed, earlier in this very year (1988) my book, *The Lost Village,* has commemorated not a village that has physically foundered but a village way of life that has irretrievably vanished into the mists of time.

But Nadderbourne, like other villages of today, is still vibrantly alive, though vastly changed. Reckoning as a newcomer someone who has put down roots within the past twenty years, 80% of the village's present inhabitants are newcomers. But the 20% residue evidently act as leaven, and the mixture is potent. The village flourishes as never before. Certainly it is far more affluent, and, while the generations I can remember would feel lost there, the present generation is contented enough.

Enough of the abiding things of the countryside survive for me to feel at home there, too. There are still skylarks unwinding their silver skein of song over the cornfields, still roseattes of primroses in the April hedgebanks, still rooks in the trees of Church Farm (though they have to nest in ash-trees since Dutch elm disease destroyed the elms), still housewives enjoying a little gossip as they meet in the village shop.

My father once greeted a newcomer with, 'Well, old man, you be come to Nadderbourne to live, and you be come to Nadderbourne to die.'

'What do you mean?'

'Well, nobody who comes to Nadderbourne ever wants to go away and die somewhere else!'

That is the village I know, and – praise be! – there are still nine thousand or more like it in England.

Ralph Whitlock
July 1988

Birth in the spring

December 1985

I was thankful that my wife's little black Pekinese, a lion-like little dog if ever there was one, relies on scent rather than sight. It was half-an-hour after sunrise on a chill November morning, with a cross-wind sweeping the woodland path free of scent. So Sammy did not smell or see the apparition that fetched me up in mid-stride, as effectively as a hand on my shoulder - a fox, sitting in the middle of the path ahead.

I lifted my field-glasses and waited for the drama to develop, ready to intervene if necessary. But Sammy was diverted by scents of wood-mice or squirrels or something at the side of the path, and the fox had other things on its mind.

On *her* mind, I should say, for a moment later another bigger fox was by her side. She nosed him, they pranced briefly around each other and then together melted into the undergrowth. They never saw me or the dog, and Sammy never saw them, though he became excited enough by the scent when he arrived at the site.

'That's the vixen I heard yelling the other evening,' I surmised, remembering the weird, unearthly screaming that had caused the hairs on the nape to rise when I was walking alone in the woods. But I may have been wrong. There are many foxes in the woods, fields, gardens and hedgerows around my home, and for some reason they are courting and mating earlier than usual this year. Most years they start about Christmas time, but I heard the eerie yell of a vixen calling for a mate before the end of October.

The gestation period of the fox is approximately fifty-three days. So if a pair of foxes mated on December 1 the cubs should be born about

January 22, and my impression is that a lot of foxes mated in November. There should therefore be many young foxes born in January, which is two months earlier than normal.

For the first fortnight the vixen stays with them in their den, and the dog fox brings her food. They do not start to take solid food until they are about a month old, but after that their progress is rapid, and they usually venture above ground in the fifth or sixth weeks of their lives.

Cubs born in mid-March are therefore ready to start exploring their world when the countryside is awaking into new life in April, but the 1986 crop will be wanting to do so in bleak February. Hard times loom ahead for some creatures, either the foxes or their prey or both.

Foxes are not among the species which have developed a technique for avoiding a winter birth-time. Badgers, stoats and martens are, and so are roe deer. Weasels, curiously enough, are not. The process, known as delayed implantation, involves a fertilised egg remaining in the female's body for months before starting to develop. Stoats, for instance, mate again soon after their young are born in spring, but, as the true gestation period is only about a month and as the next litter of young is not born until the following April, the female carries the dormant embryos for the best part of a year.

Badgers mate in spring and early summer but the embryos do not start to develop until December, when their mothers are not exactly hibernating but are spending long periods of hard weather underground, living off their fat. The rutting time for fallow deer is in October and November, but for the roe deer it is July and August. Yet because the roe deer practise delayed implantation their young are born at about the same time, in late May or June. Delayed implantation is thus demonstrated as an effective device to help a species by-pass the winter, and the wonder is that more species have not adopted it.

How encouraging it is to realise that here in England, with winter just closing in and months of unpleasant weather to come, the seeds are already sown for next spring and summer, deep in the wombs of animals as well as in the soil. For when wild gales howl across the frozen countryside, every form of life that will revel in the sunshine of midsummer is safely stowed away somewhere.

The bluebells that will carpet the woods in May are already there in embryo, in the heart of bulbs deep in the soil. Each annual flower exists well-protected by the steel-hard coating of a seed. The leaves of the oaks and beeches which will provide welcome shade next summer are neatly formed and folded tight within tightly-sealed buds. Butterflies exist in chrysalis or egg form: larvae of many other insects escape from the winter by delving deep below the frost zone; water and mud are full of dormant life.

Everything sleeping. Everything waiting. Though, as a matter of fact, some forms of life are more impatient than others. Hazel catkins are already growing and attaining half their total length. They will be scattering their pollen in the woods by the middle of January. But their tiny buds were first visible in early August.

Spring and early summer seem the natural time for new life to appear in the world. It gives young creatures the best chance of survival, during a time of abundant food before darkness and cold close in again. If therefore one reckons back from the optimum date of birth to the beginning of the gestation period, one arrives at the optimum time for mating. Which brings us back to the foxes; they have started too soon.

Late autumn is not otherwise a bad season for mating. Animals in general are well-fed, sleek and have grown a winter-coat. Farmers know this and put their ewes to the ram in November for early crops of lambs. The favoured species which use delayed implantation are able to take advantage of being in the peak of condition when the embryo starts to develop and yet are right for mating when filled with the joys of spring.

And what of the human species? You may well be familiar with the story of the country housewife who remarked that she was always glad when the primroses started to bloom and the swallows returned and the baby was born, because then she knew that spring had really arrived. A sensible rural attitude.

And when I was a boy I remember learning to chant a rhyme, used as a reproach to anyone who had a birthday in August or early September:

Betty, Betty Jarvis;
Come about in harvest!

Well, it stood to reason that no-one wanted to be bothered with newborn babies when everyone was busy with harvest. No, spring-time was the season for babies. Let them grow up with the lambs and the birds and the foxes and all the flowering and proliferating earth. I leave it to you to work backwards to establish the best and worst season for human pairing!

Heroes, idols – and celebrities

January 1986

It would be misleading to surmise that, because from time to time I converse with my long-deceased great-grandfather under the old apple-tree in the orchard where he used to set up his cider-mill, my interests are predominantly with the past. A bevy of teenage grandchildren and their friends do their best to keep me abreast of the contemporary scene, uphill work though it is for them.

I received a letter from Australia, addressed to:- 'Mr Ralph Whitlock, author and broadcaster, Wiltshire, England.' It was safely delivered. My grand-daughter was puzzled but unimpressed.

'That's because your grandad's a celebrity,' her grandmother told her.

'He is not!' was my grand-daughter's emphatic conviction.

'In the days before television he was as well known as Terry Wogan is now' declared my wife, somewhat exaggerating in her role of her husband's champion.

'But that was ages ago,' said this eighteen-year-old. 'That's history.'

Remembering a conversation I had not long ago with a distinguished old general who confessed, rather wryly, that he was now regarded as a 'geriatric nobody', I was interested to probe a little deeper into the attitudes of this new generation.

'What's a celebrity, then?' I enquired innocently.

'Well, you aren't!'

'Is Mrs Thatcher?'

'No.'

This took the wind out of my sails, for I was about to lead her backwards through a series of prime ministers until we came to a prime minister who was not a celebrity.

'Is the Queen?'

'No.' She went on to amplify this surprising answer.

'The Queen is the Queen. Mrs Thatcher is the Prime Minister. They are important and they are famous, but that isn't the same thing as being a celebrity.'

Oh dear! That brings us back to the original question. What then is a celebrity? The answer, according to these typical teenagers, is someone we know well through seeing them on television!

So now we know. A celebrity is a creation of television. And there had I been, criticising bumbling old Eamonn Andrews for saturating his ageing programme, *This is Your Life*, with show-business personalities. I had been of the opinion that he ought to introduce more explorers, mountaineers, handicapped people fighting against tremendous odds and other worthy souls, when all the time he knew best. He has been giving the public, or at least a hefty section of it, what it wants.

They have a point, though, these youngsters. Evidently they like their idols to be fairly ordinary young people like themselves - someone they can relate to. One of my young informants, whom I hope was exceptional, even criticised Bob Geldof for not being content with his role as pop idol and wanting to do something more serious with his life. Bob, as a celebrity, does not, in his view, belong to the mundane world of politicians, economists, business tycoons and other sober characters who, in fifty years' time, will have their place in history books.

Television, then, creates celebrities, as it creates many other things. It may set out simply to reflect the contemporary scene but it inevitably ends up by helping to mould it. Certainly it distorts events, even with the best of intentions. How can it be otherwise?

Today a president of an important country is assassinated; a volcano explodes; civil war flares up again in Lebanon; a Minister of the Crown is arrested for drunken driving; and a film star, high on drugs, jumps off the Eifel Tower. Troubles never come singly, as we know full well. But they all have to be fitted into the twenty-five minutes television news slot. Next week there comes a day when nothing of any great significance happens, yet the news slot still has to be filled. As Professor

Parkinson might have said, if he had waited a few years before formulating his Law, news expands (or contracts) to fill the space available for it.

Not, of course, that this is all to the bad. The magnificent response to the needs of the African famine was largely due to the publicity given by television and the Press. As the unspeakable Alf Garnett said, in discussing that very subject in a Christmas programme, 'It's all the fault of television. If they hadn't shown us all those pictures we wouldn't have known anything about it.'

The day after my encounter with my teenagers I felt the need to seek the company of my esteemed great-grandfather, under the old apple-tree.

'Who were your heroes when you were a boy?' I asked him.

He had to think for several minutes.

'Well, I mind old Steppy Garner, who could throw a cricket ball from the cricket pitch right out of the field and into the allotments. Now how far would that be? Two or three hundred yards?'

'No-no, not that sort of man ...'

'And I once saw Billy Adlam drink a yard of cider in less than a minute ...'

'No-no. Someone you read about in the papers or heard other people talking about.'

'We never had any papers.'

No, of course not. Not only no television and no radio but no papers, except one restricted local one every Thursday. So who would they have heard about on the national scene? Gladstone? Yes. The local MP? Yes.

'David Livingstone, we knew about him. He was exploring Africa in my time. And General Gordon. And Florence Nightingale.'

'What about famous actors and entertainers?'

Silly question. How could he have ever heard of them? He never went to London in his life; probably never to a theatre.

I came from the orchard, pondering. How much better informed our present generation of teenagers is! It is perhaps futile to ask oneself whether they are either better or worse for that - to me they seem much the same as teenagers have always been - but it may be legitimate to query the choice of idols being presented to them, created for them by television.

They've never had it so good

March 1984

My morning walk takes me through varied countryside. I follow lanes, field tracks, and woodland rides as well as a section of suburbia which used to be the tail-end of our village.

Mechanical hedge-cutters have given the hedges by the lanes such a ruthless trimming ('short back and sides' describes it pretty accurately) that they no longer offer worthwhile shelter to anything larger than a beetle, if that. Old hedges that I remember in the arable fields have been hurtled into oblivion by bulldozer disease, leaving an unrelieved 'desert' of cereal crops. The woodland rides are ruler-straight lines between regimented ranks of conifers responsible for such deep shade that even on a sunny summer afternoon the woodland floor has only a carpet of last year's discarded needles.

It is the sort of landscape calculated to make the hackles rise on any self-respecting conservationist. 'What have they done to our lovely countryside? ' is a lament I can well understand and appreciate. But an inspection of details does not always substantiate the claims about rape and ruin.

In my garden before I begin my walk I see more birds and more species of birds than over almost all the rest of the course. There are sparrows, starlings, chaffinches, greenfinches, collared doves, robins, hedge-sparrows, blackbirds, a singing thrush, magpies, great tits, blue tits and coal tits, often a wood pigeon or two, a pair of mistle-thrushes, sometimes a wren and sometimes a pied wagtail, as well as occasional birds of passage in the migration seasons. Needless to say, I have a well patronised bird table, constantly supplied with peanuts and scraps.

Now these are all birds which, in the days before humans started to make a mess of the environment, would have been birds of the woodland margins. Their homes and refuges would have been in the low bushes that fringed the trees, from which haven they would have darted out into the clearings for morsels of food and back again before any predator could pounce on them. The population of any area the size of my garden would have been far less than the pensioners that I attract.

The establishment of human settlements provided pickings for avian hangers-on but at the expense of increased hazards. When I was a boy, in the 1920s, all those birds which now feast with impunity in my garden would have lived much more dangerous lives. I had first a catapult and then an airgun, with which I wrought deeds of which I am now ashamed, though no-one then told me that I was doing wrong. We village boys had a well-tried technique of killing blackbirds in hedgerows, taking advantage of the blackbird's reluctance to fly or to move into the tops of the bushes. We were adept at catching finches by night by the ruse of holding a torch behind a vertical net on one side of a tall hedge and beating the other side of the hedge with sticks. We used to make nocturnal forays to extract sparrows and tits from their roosting places under the eaves of the abundant thatched roofs. Blackbirds, thrushes and other birds of that size were plucked and used in pies.

Our sharp eyes made us expert at finding birds' nests, and robins' eggs were the only ones safe from us - and that only because we had been told that if we took them our little fingers would grow crooked. In our district we had no tradition of Garland Day in May, but if there had been we would have been only too willing to adorn our May garlands with birds' eggs as well as flowers, smashing them with stones at the end of the festival, as happened in many other places. Lapwings' eggs were a prized find, providing as they did a tasty breakfast.

We were, of course, only taking our cue from the adults of our community, who had little to learn about methods of shooting, trapping and snaring wild creatures. A bird was good to eat or it was an enemy of the pampered pheasant; either way it got killed. Many a time on a woodland walk on an afternoon after Sunday School my attention has been caught by the raucous and desperate cries of a jay caught in a pole trap, that most hideous of all gins. No-one told us that the dreadful contraption was evil, though our innate compassion said that it must be. All birds with hooked beaks and sharp talons were supposed to be detrimental to human interests, which condemned the harmless kestrel and barn owl together with certain less innocent species.

Nor were attitudes more enlightened in earlier ages. Before the era of firearms the birds had a better chance, but the human genius for destruction is versatile and highly inventive. Decoys, nets, and bird lime encompassed the doom of myriads of victims. Even as late as the 1920s most of the cottagers in our village kept wild birds, such as goldfinches and bullfinches, in tiny cages, the supply being constantly replenished by the local bird-catcher.

The record dated 1271 which decreed that the chief forester of the Forest of Delamere, in Cheshire, was entitled to all sparrow-hawks, merlins, and hobbies in the Forest is a reminder of not only another method of killing birds before the invention of gunpowder but also that the hawks used for the sport were taken as nestlings from the nests of wild birds.

Compare the lot of birds in such minefields of hazards with that of the favoured company that feed in my garden, and in countless similar gardens. Or with the immunity from persecution of the kestrels nesting on tall city buildings, of the wild duck nesting in roof gardens in central London, of the Arctic wildfowl wintering in city parks and of the blackbirds which revel in urban and suburban life.

Every hawk and owl and most other birds are on the protected list. People have become more civilised, more humane, more tolerant and less addicted to spreading death and mayhem all around them, and by their increasing boldness the birds show that they know it.

The ultimate example of confidence in this newfound immunity was provided for me by a wood pigeon in Plymouth. My car was first in a queue of traffic drawn up at traffic lights near the city centre. This bird, walking along the road, came to the edge, looked up at the lights and then at the waiting traffic, and then, having assessed the situation, calmly walked across the pedestrian crossing rather than take wing and fly to the other side of the road!

All is not perfect on the conservation front, but, by and large, birds have never had it so good.

A nice cup of tea

April 1984

When in the bleak autumn of 1620 the Pilgrim Fathers disembarked from *The Mayflower* and began setting up house at 'New Plimouth' one of their laments was that they had to drink cold spring water because they had run short of beer. 'Bring beer, and plenty of it,' was their advice in reports back to colleagues in England who were contemplating joining them.

This sounds somewhat strange to us who have been used to equating the Pilgrims with the Nonconformists of later times and their rigid regard for the principle of total abstinence.

But what choice had they? It wasn't until after the Restoration of Charles II in 1660 that the importation of tea to England began. Before that time the standard beverages, even for women and children, were beer, ale and cider, and no doubt they were a good deal safer than the average polluted water supply. When travelling in some of the more remote and primitive corners of the world I myself have more than once thought it wise to clean my teeth with lager.

It took about a hundred years for tea-drinking to become thoroughly established in England, but by the end of the eighteenth century 'in poor families, tea was not only the usual beverage in the morning and evening but was generally drunk in large quantities at dinner.' Still, that was only about two hundred years ago, so tea as an almost universal beverage can claim only two centuries out of the long roll-call of English history.

Now it seems that its era may be drawing to a close. India no longer has a surplus of tea for export, on account of vastly increased home consumption, and other tea-producing countries, such as Kenya, are finding good alternative markets in Japan and elsewhere. So prices are rising and may soon take wing.

Common Market grape-growers would doubtless like us to replace tea by wine, while enthusiastic advocates of milk stout and malt whisky can always be found. Beer and ale are still readily available, and West Countrymen have long been noted for their loyalty to cider. But there are other alternatives. Tea is technically a tisane - an infusion of dried herbs - and there are other dried herbs which can be used in the same way.

Some of them can, in fact, be purchased at health food shops. Camomile tea, for instance, is prepared in exactly the same way as ordinary tea and has a pleasant, aromatic flavour. I often drink it, though, like other herb teas, it is best without milk but with the addition of lemon juice.

Lemon balm tea is probably best made from fresh rather than dried leaves, though bear in mind that about twice as much of chopped fresh leaves is required to make the same amount of beverage. Put a handful of them in a pot, preferably a glass one, and boil for about five minutes. Sweeten with honey rather than sugar.

Plants of the Labiate family, which includes mints of various kinds, marjoram, basil and sage, make excellent tisanes. As a child I was regularly dosed with hot mint tea at bedtime to ward off winter ills, though now I think that iced mint tea on hot summer days is better. A tea made from dried raspberry leaves is reputed to have saved my life during one bout of infantile illness, though in those primitive days one cannot be sure that the credit was rightly bestowed.

The incident does serve to indicate, however, that many, perhaps most, of the herbal tisanes were valued for their supposed or real medicinal properties rather than simply as pleasant drinks. Horehound tea, made from the white horehound (a labiate herb), is supposed to be a cure for colds. An infusion of agrimony helps digestion and is good for liver complaints. Rosemary tea is a remedy for headaches. An infusion made from mallow flowers helps to heal an ulcerated mouth or throat.

So the tally goes on. I accept no responsibility for the efficacy or otherwise of any of the alleged remedies, but all of them can be enjoyed apart from the good they are supposed to do you. Most of them tend to be bitter, though that may be regarded as by no means an undesirable quality in an iced drink in summer, and it can be disguised by honey if taken hot.

Considered purely as beverages there is much to be said for concoctions of mixed herbs, and as there are at least fifty varieties of herbs and other plants suitable for use in infusions the permutations are almost limitless. A 'country house-wife', writing in 1753, recommended a mixture of aniseed, sweet fennel, cinquefoil, mallow roots, fennel roots, figs and raisins, boiled for a quarter of an hour, strained and sweetened with sugar-candy.

What sounds a somewhat more appetising drink is a herb punch based on ginger ale (3 quarts) and tea (one quart) to which a handful or two each of borage, lemon balm, mint and the juice of lemons and oranges have been added. Serve iced.

Perhaps the most useful idea of all is to use herb tisanes to eke out supplies of ordinary tea. Put the tea leaves into a jar or pot and cover with about an equal quantity of the fresh leaves or flowers of some herb, such as mint, fragrant geranium, balm, lemon verbena. Stir up the contents of the jar daily until all the fresh material has dried and has been thoroughly mixed with the tea.

The economics of the process may appeal to some, for almost all the herbs can be easily grown in the garden. Some of them, like lemon balm, are little better than weeds; once they have become established it is tremendously difficult to get rid of them. At least in our search for alternative beverages we need not fall back on the somewhat desperate recipe I heard recommended by a Central African housewife at the end of a course at a mission school.

Being, like so many African women, capable of making a speech at the drop of a hat, she was eloquently extolling the virtues of red beetroot, a crop to which she had been recently introduced. (And, incidentally, in England in bygone years beetroot was reckoned to be a remedy for anaemia). Having given her audience little cubes of beet, grown in her own garden, she went on, 'And when towards the end of the week your husband demands a drink and you have no money left, you need not submit to a beating because you cannot offer him anything. No, you will give him this.'

She produced glasses of what looked like a lovely, cooling, strawberry-flavoured milk-shake, ideal for thirst-quenching under the hot afternoon sun. Ugh! It was lukewarm goat's-milk flavoured with beetroot juice! My wife had to drink hers up and then make a speech congratulating the class on their ingenuity and achievement. While she was doing so I quietly emptied my horrid drink on the grass behind my back!

Whither education?

February 1984

Some months had elapsed since I last had a chat with my long deceased great-grandfather under the old apple-tree down the orchard, where he used to set up his cider press, but after Christmas I felt impelled to seek him out. I wanted to ask him whether in his time he had ever experienced feelings of inadequacy in the presence of the younger generation.

Knowing eyes were focused on me from beneath bushy grey eyebrows. 'Trouble with grandchildren?' he enquired. 'Yes,' I told him. 'They had computers for Christmas.' The intelligent eyes took on a glazed expression. 'Computers? What are they?'

How to explain computers to a man whose span of life on earth ended in 1882?

'The ones my grandsons have work through a television screen ...' I began, and then realised that he had no idea what a television screen is. 'It's all to do with electronics ...' I started again and was immediately at a loss for words.

'The fact is, you don't know, isn't it?' my great-grandfather interrupted, 'and your grandchildren do!'

'That's exactly it,' I nodded agreement. 'Even little kids six and eight years old understand these things better than I do. And as for the teenagers ...'

He sighed. 'I know just how you feel,' he assured me. 'Youngsters always have been too clever by half...'

'When I was a boy,' he reminisced, 'my parents sent me to a dame's school. The dame was a Mrs Anne Scroggins, whose husband had got himself killed in the wars with Napoleon. At least, that was her story. We used to sit on stools in her front room - for she was a very genteel lady who had a front room - and write on slates. The little girls sewed samplers - you know, the alphabet and their names and some Scripture texts on squares of cloth. One of the little girls, named Elizabeth, was Mrs Scroggins' daughter. She was two years younger than me, and later on I married her and she became your great-grandmother.

'My father used to pay twopence a week for my schooling, and often enough he had a job to find that. So I didn't have many years at school. About four, I think, though of course I missed a lot of time, helping with haymaking, harvest and so on, in summer. The dame concentrated on the basics. When I left, when I was about eleven, I could read, write, spell and do adding, subtracting, multiplying and dividing sums, and that was about all. How long do they spend at school now?'

'Oh, they start when they're four or five and carry on till they're sixteen, as a rule - sometimes a good deal longer if they go in for further education.'

'Well, there you are! I had four years at school; my children had about seven, and now your lot have eleven or twelve or a bit more. No wonder they're better educated and make you feel inadequate.'

I pondered this. 'They can't spell,' I told him sadly, thinking of some of the mistakes in the latest letter from one of my grandchildren now living overseas – 'niether', 'prikely', 'pritty', 'dispare', 'are' instead of 'our', 'neet', 'teridactiles' (pterodactyls).

'Well, some people never can seem to learn spelling,' said my great-grandfather, philosophically. 'Are they good at sums?'

'No.'

'I used to be quite good at sums,' he reminisced. 'I could do any ordinary multiplication and division in my head.'

'Well, they can't. They don't even know their tables. They have pocket calculators even to do simple addition sums.'

'Pocket calculators?'

'Another device to make things easy for them. All they have to do is to press the right buttons and the correct answer appears.'

My great-grandfather was in a tolerant mood. 'Well, if they have to learn about these computers, which even you don't understand, I dare say they need all the time and short cuts they can get.'

I forebore to mention Parkinson's Law, formulated since his time but true in every age, that *Work expands to fill the time available to it,* because he went on, 'After all, there must be some wonderful careers open to them after eleven or twelve years of that sort of education.'

'For some of them,' I agreed, 'but half of them can't get jobs at all.'

'Well, then, see how well they are equipped for leisure,' said this optimistic old-timer. 'My wife was better educated than me, being a schoolteacher's daughter, and she took me in hand a bit after we were married. In the winter evenings there was nothing much to do, out on the farm where we lived, so she made me read a lot, and I got to like it. I read all the classics, like Dickens, and Scott and Thackeray, and I learned to play the old harmonium, and I taught myself shorthand. I was pretty good at figures, so they made me secretary of the Pig Club and then Parish Clerk, and I was chairman of the local Liberal Party, which was strong about here in those days. Not bad for a man who had less than four years at school, eh? But I could have done with some of the opportunities these youngsters get nowadays. I did have to spend most of my life ploughing fields and mucking out pigs and mowing grass and milking cows and castrating lambs and pressing cider under this here old apple-tree, after all. I wish I had had more time for other things. And I reckon I would have mastered those computers, even if you can't!'

A fat lot of comfort I got from my chat with my great-grandfather down the orchard.

New lambs of Candlemas

January 1982

Outside the Roman Catholic Church, Candlemas Day, February 2, now has little significance in Britain. In the ecclesiastical calendar it is the feast of the Purification of the Virgin Mary, referring to the ancient custom which required a mother to offer candles on her first visit to church after childbirth. Actually it supersedes a much older pagan festival, the feast of Imbolc.

A Celtic quarter-day in pre-Christian Britain, Imbolc belongs to a pastoral calendar which preceded the agricultural one with its quarter-days on Lady Day, Midsummer, Michaelmas, and Christmas. Imbolc was important in marking the traditional beginning of the lambing season. Although the name is largely forgotten, the date retains some of its old significance for farming communities, as the time when the earliest lambs are born.

The first week of February, when some of the worst winter weather can be expected, may seem a particularly inclement season for starting lambing, but there are good reasons. Lambs born then are just the right age in April and May to make full use of the spring grass. What is even more important to the sheep farmer, they are ready for marketing, as fat lambs, in early July, when prices are at their peak. So February lambs are worth the extra trouble. That extra trouble is considerable. Ewes lambing in April can be allowed to drop their lambs on the open pastures with little attention, but in February they need warmth, shelter, and individual care. On the farm where I was reared in the 1920s, preparations for the lambing took priority over everything else in the weeks leading up to Candlemas Day.

The lambing pen was a large enclosure, its walls composed of double rows of wattle hurdles, the space between them being stuffed with straw. It was sited to take maximum advantage of whatever natural shelter was available, such as the angle of two tall hedges in a valley. Often in the previous autumn a straw rick was built there, partly to provide ample straw for littering the pen but also as an additional windbreak.

The pen was divided into four parts - one for the ewes before lambing, one for ewes and newly born lambs, one for ewes with twins or triplets, and one for the ewes and lambs after the lambs were a week or so old. Sections two and three, smaller than the others and occupying the cosiest site against the hedge or the straw rick, were sub-divided. Their walls were lined with 'coops', which were small compartments one hurdle square, with another couple of hurdles heaped with straw to act as a roof.

Beyond the outer sections of the pen was a turnip-field, where the expectant mothers fed by day. And in a sheltered corner just outside the pen was the shepherd's hut. In this wooden box mounted on iron wheels were a stove, a table and chair, a ledge piled with clothes which served as a bed, one or two shelves holding medicines, tools and provisions, and a deep chest packed with hay. In the stove a fire burned day and night. The shepherd lived here for about six weeks, inspecting the flock at hourly intervals during the night though taking an occasional nap by day, when someone was on hand to relieve him.

As soon as a lamb was born the shepherd placed it with its mother in one of the coops, on an ample bed of straw, and would not leave it until it was healthily sucking. In severe weather a newly-born lamb would sometimes be found half-dead with cold and weakness. Its limp body was then buried in the hay-box in front of the stove, the hay pressed around it until it seemed that the little animal must suffocate. But the treatment was usually effective.

Ewes with twins and triplets were provided with a pen of their own because they earned the shepherd a bonus. Most farmers offered a shilling or so for every lamb reared above the number of ewes in the flock.

Lambs destined for the early summer market are still born around

Candlemas Day and still need to be cossetted and pampered in much the same way as in the past. Most farmers who follow this system of sheep-farming now, however, bring their ewes into permanent buildings just before lambing. Spacious, multi-purpose buildings can be erected with the help of Government grants, but the internal arrangements are similar to those in the old-time lambing pens.

In recent years some farmers who lack convenient buildings have been hiring big marquees, of the sort used for farm shows and village fetes, for the lambing period. These huge tents are equipped with piped water and electricity, making life more comfortable for sheep and shepherds alike.

To be strictly accurate, one should mention shepherdesses, for girls are often auxiliaries in the modern lambing pen. Midwifery is, after all, traditionally women's work, and caring for newborn lambs is a task at which girls seem to excel.

Shadow of the moon

September 1987

Analysing humour is as thankless a task as trying to explain a joke to a person who has failed three times to appreciate the point of it. So when I read that a paper on *The Irish Joke as a Social Phenomenon* was to be given at the annual meeting of the British Association for the Advancement of Science I offered a little prayer of thanksgiving that I would not be required to be in the audience.

Most countries evidently tend to tell derogatory jokes about certain of their neighbours. Christie Davies, Professor of Sociology at Reading University, says that just as we enjoy our Irish jokes, so the Americans concoct jokes about Poles, the Russians about Ukrainians, the Swedes about the Finns, the Australians about the Tasmanians, and the Irish themselves about the people of Kerry.

Says the professor: 'The butts are either the closest and most familiar of neighbours, the most remote and provincial of their own people, or long-established and half-assimilated minorities.' That statement rang a bell. Here in Wiltshire we take pleasure in referring to Hampshire Hogs, Somerset Cuckoos, Devonshire Dumplings (or is it Dorset Dumplings?) and the rest.

Zummerzet born; Zummerzet bred;
Strong in th' arm, an' thick in the haid.

That sort of thing.

And, of course, in Wiltshire we have the tale of the Wiltshire Moonrakers, which can be taken as typical. For readers who do not happen to know it, let me briefly recount the story.

One moonlit autumn night two hundred or so years ago some travellers spotted two or three Wiltshiremen dragging hay-rakes through a roadside pond. On being asked what they were doing, the yokels pointed to the reflection of the full moon and explained.

'See! There be a gurt yaller cheese in thik pond and we be goin' to rake en out!

The travellers went on their way laughing at 'they there dunder-headed coons, a-reakin after the shadder of the moon!

Of course, any Wiltshireman can recite the true version of events. The travellers were excisemen, looking for smugglers. The 'yokels' were smugglers, handling casks of contraband brandy. Spotting the approach of the excisemen they rolled their barrels out of the cart and into the pond. When they thought the danger was past they started to try to retrieve their load but became so engrossed in the exercise that they failed to notice the customs officers returning.

Originally the story belonged not to all Wiltshire but to the village of Bishop's Cannings, in the middle of the county. And, for some reason, a whole constellation of similar tales have clustered like a colony of barnacles around this long-suffering village.

One evening, so neighbouring villages said, the entire population of Bishop's Cannings turned up in Devizes market-place. They had heard that a comet was due to appear, so they had come to town to see it. An embellishment to the tale is that one farm worker brought his rick-ladder, to set up against his waggon so that he could get a better view.

When they noticed that some of their neighbours had taller spires to their churches than they did they piled farmyard manure around theirs to make it grow. When the heap began to sink they exclaimed: 'There! He be growin' up fine!

And when a gardener at the Vicarage saw a strange dog biting at the handle of his wheelbarrow he immediately sawed off the handle, for fear of hydrophobia.

It was decided to revive the Bishop's Cannings Band, and a diligent search revealed assorted musical instruments in cottages, pigsties and even in the church vestry. The vestry seemed as good a place as any for band practice, so the musicians met there weekly until they felt confident enough to appear at the village fete.

Then they made a disconcerting discovery. Since the days of the previous band, a new door had been fitted to the vestry, and it was too narrow to allow the big drum to pass through. So the drummer sat in the vestry, beating out the time, while the band marched round the village.

Why should such an inoffensive little village attract such a collection

of insulting tales?

In the times of King James I the parish had a minister, a Mr Ferraby, who was an excellent and enterprising musician. He trained a choir of his parishioners, who 'sung the Psalmes in consort to the organ, which Mr Ferraby procured to be erected. When King James was in these parts .... he entertained His Majesty with bucoliques of his own making and composing, sung by the parishioners .... The eight bells, of which he was the cause, did ring and the organ played on.'

The musical programme was followed by a football match, and it was said that the parish 'could have challenged all England for musique, football and ringing.'

Later Mr Ferraby staged a similar performance for Queen Anne, wife of James I.

Well, it's obvious, isn't it? All this went to the heads of the Bishop's Cannings people, who had to be taken down a peg, and there's none so efficient as neighbours for doing just that. Mr Ferraby could compose his bucoliques, but they didn't last as long as the scurrilous tales invented by the neighbours.

The ominous magotty-pie

November 1987

Magpies are evidently far less plentiful in the western states of America than here, for the sight of one recently prompted a Seattle reader to write to tell me. She recalls that in England last summer she was told that one was supposed to recite a rhyme, for luck, when seeing a magpie. She wanted to know more about this and any superstitions relating to magpies and other birds and animals. That opens a very wide door indeed.

An old Scots woman is alleged to have said she would 'sooner see the devil than a magpie on that tree,' indicating a tree near her home. It was a bird of ill omen, and I feel sure there were incantations to avert the bad luck it was supposed to bring. So far, however, I have been unable to find anyone who remembers them, and if any readers are able to relieve my ignorance I shall be pleased to hear from them.

One rhyme which is still familiar to most country folk is:

One for sorrow,
Two for mirth,
Three for a wedding,
Four for a birth.

But in all matters pertaining to magpies there is contradiction. According to one version, the last line runs *Four for a death.*

My great-grandfather, William, whom I have consulted about it, assured me that it is lucky to see a single magpie but unlucky to see more. But in his day magpies were not as abundant in England as they are now; on my daily walks I normally see at least three or four and often more.

Great-grandmother Elizabeth, however, did add that you can avert any ill-luck by turning round three times. And she knew a different interpretation from that quoted above. According to her, while a sight of one magpie denoted sorrow, two together foretold gaiety or perhaps a wedding; three, a successful journey; four, an unexpected piece of good news; five or more, that you would shortly find yourself in enjoyable company.

Two or three magpies chattering around a house were supposed to indicate the arrival of strangers; though according to another version they presaged a violent quarrel between husband and wife. In some quarters they seem to have been regarded as a favourable omen, for it is on record that the persistent chattering of magpies on the site encouraged a noble Saxon lady to persuade her husband to found a monastery at Osney, in Oxfordshire.

Alexander Nickham, a writer on medieval England, states that it was considered an advantage to have a pair of magpies nesting in a poultry yard, because their chattering would give warning of a thief, but this seems to me unlikely. The magpies would probably take a heavier toll of eggs than any thief.

A lullaby of about a hundred years ago gives a typical unfavourable view of the magpie:

Hush-a-bye, babby,
The beggar shan't have 'ee,
Nor shall the magotty-pie [magpie]
The rook nor the raven
Shan't car' [carry] thee to heaven,
So hush-a-bye, babby, bye-bye.

The name 'magpie', incidentally, is formed simply by attaching a familiar forename to a descriptive word. 'Pie is the equivalent of 'pied' – black-and-white and 'Mag' was a well known abbreviation of a Christian name, Margaret, used here as in Tom-tit, Jenny-wren and Robin redbreast.

The allusion seems to me to throw light on a curious nonsense tale attached to certain English villages, one of which is Piddinghoe, in Sussex. In a recent article I quoted some tales associated with Bishops Cannings, the birthplace of the Wiltshire Moonraker legend. Well, Piddinghoe has a similar collection of yarns, one of them being that its inhabitants 'shod magpies', explained by the fact that locally the black-and-white oxen employed for ploughing a hundred years ago were known as 'magpies'.

Oddly enough, another tall story from Piddinghoe is that the villagers were addicted to 'fishing for the moon' and 'digging for moonshine'; although I was at first astonished when a Yorkshire reader, after reading my recent account of the Wiltshire Moonrakers, introduced me to the 'Slowit Moonrakers', I soon realised that the story was more widespread than I had thought.

At one time the Huddersfield Narrow Canal ran through Slaithwaite town centre and broadened out into 'Slowit Docks'. There smugglers were accustomed to lowering casks of brandy into the water and fishing them out at dead of night. When challenged they 'played gormless' and insisted they were only raking the moon out of the canal. And I'm told that nearby there is now a bistro named 'The Moonraker'.

Hedgehogs, hares and hernias

December 1987

'What about hedgehogs?' challenges a reader, prompted by my recent cogitations about magpies. They indeed seem to have attracted more than their fair share of country superstitions, and to have suffered in consequence.

I cannot believe, though, that the old allegation that hedgehogs invade orchards in order to roll on the fallen apples and carry them off on their spines ever originated in the countryside. Any countryman, especially if he had skinned and eaten a hedgehog, would know that, although the spines are firmly attached to the skin, the skin is so loose that the weight of any fair-sized apple could not be supported. Even more decisive is the fact that the hedgehog is an insectivore and has no use for apples.

More controversial is the tale that hedgehogs suck the milk from cows. I have often discussed this with old farmers and labourers, some of whom have sworn they have seen hedgehogs at work on the udders of cows sitting on grass and chewing the cud. The explanantion could well be that the hedgehogs were lapping up milk oozing from the full udder of a freshly-calved cow, as can happen when she is sitting down.

Hedgehogs certainly like milk, as is demonstrated by the avidity with which a garden hedgehog will devour bread-and-milk. Or, on the other hand, the hedgehogs allegedly sucking cows could have been snapping up worms and insects around the cows' warm bodies. But a hedgehog's jaws are not built to fit around a cow's teat.

Cud-chewing cows were also at risk from shrews, according to rural folklore. An aunt of mine, who died at the age of nearly ninety in 1966, used to call shrews 'over-runners'. By scampering over a recumbent cow, she claimed, they caused her milk to dry up. To have a shrew run over your foot would bring exceptionally bad luck, a superstition which comes within the realm of witchcraft. The corrective treatment was to bore a hole in an ash tree, insert a live shrew and seal it with a plug. As the shrew died and decayed, so the ill-luck would fade away. Gilbert White was familiar with this tradition at Selborne two hundred years ago.

Incidentally, a shrew-ash is different from a split ash. A shrew-ash was a mature tree, used for the purpose time and again, but a split ash had to be a sapling that had never been cut since it emerged from a seed. Based on the notion of sympathetic medicine, it was used to cure a hernia in a child.

A cleft two or three feet long was made in the upright ash and levered open wide enough for the naked body of the child to be passed through it. The ceremony had to be performed in the early morning, when the dew still stood on the grass, and required the services of a girl and a boy. The girl, standing on the eastern side of the tree, passed the child through the slit to the boy on the western. In some versions, this had to be done three times. The ash sapling was then bound together, and as it healed so would the child's rupture. There is an association with witches here, too, for ash twigs were a well-known protection against witchcraft.

Did you know that to cut your toe-nails while sitting under an ash-tree is a cure for toothache? I digress. To return to the shrews, my aunt also knew that the bite of a shrew was poisonous. Or so she maintained. It was, she said quite painful, and the effects lasted about a week.

For a long time naturalists put this down as an old wives' tale, but in the 1940s an American scientist, intrigued by hearing similar stories in his country, took the trouble to investigate and found, to general surprise, that the shrew's saliva *was* venomous. Apparently the toxic substance is manufactured by the animal's submaxillary gland and is strong enough to kill a mouse within minutes.

The experiment was conducted on American shrews and, as far as I know, has not been repeated with European species, but it seems reasonable to suppose that the results would be similar. My aunt would not have been impressed at being thus vindicated; she was one of those who *knew*.

My great-grandfather William, whom I meet from time to time under the old apple-tree down the orchard, where he used to set up his cider-press every autumn, has assured me that pigs can see the wind. He looked upon larks with disfavour because they used their long hind claw to pierce the brain of a sheep and give it the disorder which he termed 'the giddy'. He believed that keeping guinea-fowl in the farmyard would drive rats away, but I have never found anything to substantiate that strange theory.

When his brother, a notorious poacher (as most villagers were in those days), was old and frail he heard a noise in his cottage kitchen and tottered out to find a hare had ventured inside. He knew then that his time had come and, taking to his bed, was dead within a few days. For a hare to enter a building, besides being most unusual, was extremely bad luck.

Though he often included hares among his poaching trophies, my great-grandfather never ate them. Great-grandmother would not let him. 'It would be like cannibalism,' she declared. Hares, sacred animals in the pre-Christian religion of these islands, were reputed to be interchangeable with witches. 'Who knows? Put a hare in the stew and we might be eating old Biddy Burges,' was great-grandmother's opinion.

The suspect chalice

April 1987

Misgivings that some congregations are having about taking Communion wine, for fear of becoming infected by AIDS, brings to mind the story of a similar scare in an English village 170 years ago.

In the congregation was a somewhat uncouth character with lip cancer. So the pastor took the opportunity afforded by the 250th anniversary of the place of worship to replace the ancient chalice by a set of individual glasses. This was Horningsham Old Meeting House, on the edge of the Marquess of Bath's Longleat estate in Wiltshire. Its claim that the celebrations of 1816 marked its 250th anniversary makes it the oldest nonconformist place of worship in England.

The story of its foundation is that in the England of Queen Elizabeth I a band of itinerant Scottish masons, with their wives and children, were trudging from place to place, offering their skill to the new Tudor gentry who were busy replacing medieval monastic buildings with mansions in the renaissance style. In 1566 they arrived at Horningsham, where Sir John Thynne was planning the palatial Longleat House on the site of an old priory.

Engaged to work on the project, they settled in a place still called 'Little Scotland'. As Presbyterians, they were accustomed to persecution and so on the Sabbath thought it prudent to worship secretly, in a copse known as Penny's Wood. Sir John, however, was well disposed towards Protestantism, having been prominent in public life during the recent reign of the Protestant boy-king, Edward VI. Hearing of these conventicles, he offered the Scots the lease of land to build for themselves a meeting-house. One tradition says that he himself paid for it.

The building they erected is said to be the one that survives to this day, and a date deeply carved in a stone set in the west wall makes the claim. If that is true, though any documentary evidence has long since vanished, it is the oldest Protestant chapel in England, probably in the world, and the oldest nonconformist place of worship still in regular use.

It is a low, thatched building, in as lovely a setting as could be found in all England. Behind it, towering wooded hills provide a view known to holiday-makers as Heaven's Gate - a magnificent view of parkland and meadow, lakes and streams. You could easily slip through the tiny village, though, without noticing it, for it stands below the level of the road, and access is by way of a worn and sloping cobbled path, known as The Batch.

The interior is plain and fairly modern, for a vigorous renovation scheme in 1863 demolished most of the old furnishings, including the old box pews. The dark oak pulpit, with a sounding board, stands on a pedestal and is flanked by two old brass candlesticks, all that remain of those which used to provide winter illumination for the chapel. The galleries, however, were not interfered with.

On one side sat the young men, with their hats hanging from still extant wooden pegs; opposite them sat the girls, and in the end gallery, facing the pulpit, the choir grouped themselves around the musicians. Their chief instruments were reputedly the bass viol and the flute.

Far from any other Presbyterian place of worship, Horningsham Old Meeting House was for many years classified as Independent, though later it became associated with the Congregational Union. The earliest minister of whom there is any record was an American, Rowland Cotton, who was born in New Hampshire in 1674 and who, having qualified as a doctor, settled in the town of Warminster, next door to Longleat, about 1701. Being brought up as an Independent, he was soon worshipping with the Horningsham congregation and served with them, as their leader and minister (unpaid!) for nearly forty years.

The chapel has always been to some extent protected by the descendants of Sir John Thynne at Longleat. Once, in the eighteenth century, the Earl of Weymouth at Longleat was requested by the local parson to eject the Old Meeting House minister, on the grounds that his chapel was drawing people away from the parish church. Having made enquiries, the Earl invited the minister to dinner, asked him to say grace, had an enjoyable conversation with him, and sent him away with a new lease of the chapel and attached cottage in his pocket, as well as a donation.

Earlier, in 1670, an elder of the Horningsham congregation, Jeremy Cray, was fined for attending a conventicle nearby, in defiance of the Act of Uniformity but eighteen years later was appointed High Sheriff of Wiltshire.

And what of that suspect Communion plate? When it was replaced by the new set in 1816 it seems to have been acquired by the Reverend Joseph Silcox, of Frome, who emigrated to Canada in 1829. And when I researched this little byway of history a few years ago I located it in Ontario! It had been passed down from generation to generation until the last of the Silcox family gave a few of the vessels to the United Church at Frome, Ontario, (a township which Joseph Silcox had helped to found), and the rest to the Elgin County Historical Museum in St Thomas, about seven miles distant.

There they still are, carefully preserved and displayed - a treasured memento in the New World of the oldest Free Church in England.

Village democracy – the annual general meeting

January 1986

'The Annual General Meeting of the Nadderbourne Cricket Club was held at 7 o'clock last Thursday evening in the Village Hall. This was unfortunate, as most of the members arrived at 7.30, as erroneously advertised in the previous issue of this paper...'

So began a news item in the parish magazine which my brother and I, as teenagers, produced for a time in the 1930s. A chance perusal of the now yellowing pages recently served to remind me that the period between Christmas and Easter was, and indeed still is, the conventional season for annual general meetings of local organisations.

The Cricket Club, the Youth Club, the Horticultural Society, the Young Farmers' Club, sundry church organisations, and the Parish Council all arranged their annual business meetings during the dark, frosty evenings of January, February and early March, when everyone could huddle comfortably around the 'tortoise' slow combustion stove in our village hall.

'Village Hall', I call it, to give it the more exalted title its successor now bears, but in the inter-war years, when it was simply a surplus timber hut from World War One, it was known as the Reading Room. The only village organisations which did not make use of its facilities for their AGMs were the church ones, which shivered in the vestry, and the Parish Council, which, for some unexplained reason, felt constrained to patronise the village school.

And good fun we editors had, peering through the windows and afterwards depicting the antics of staid, stiff and broad-beamed parish councillors fitting themselves into and trying to ease themselves out of the little low chairs designed for the infant class.

On the occasion of the aforementioned Cricket Club AGM no great harm was done by the late arrival of most of the members. The office-holders of the previous year, having their own source of information, turned up at the proper time, which meant they were ready to start soon after 7.15.

The chairman, having decided to begin, instructed the Secretary to read the minutes, 'and read 'em slowly', he exhorted, in a stage whisper, 'and perhaps there'll be more of us here by the time you've finished.' Which is what happened.

The agenda for the meeting followed a familiar pattern. After the minutes, the main items were (a) the election of officers, (b) the fixture list and (c) finance.

Under the first heading the election of the President was a formality, the honour inevitably falling to the farmer who allowed us to use one of his meadows as a playing-field, free of charge. The bevy of Vice-Presidents comprised anyone locally whom we thought might send us a subscription.

Foremost among the active officers was the Captain, for which position, it might be thought, there would be considerable rivalry. And so there would have been, for most of the leading players would have liked to order the rest about, decide on the batting order, and keep themselves on bowling far longer than their skills warranted.

But there was a snag. No matter what arrangements were made and good resolutions passed in January or February, everyone knew that the man who would mow and mark out the pitch on Friday nights or Saturday mornings from May onwards would be the Captain! At various times the experiment of drawing up a rota for ground preparation had been tried, and the AGM had seen everyone promising to take his share, but somehow, by mid-season, the captain was keeping his solitary vigil with lawnmower and whitening-pot as usual.

The Secretary's post, too, was not an envied one. Apart from writing flattering letters to the President and Vice-Presidents, his immediate duty was to prepare a fixture list. As our club was never of sufficient calibre to enrol in any league, all our matches were friendlies, or, to be more precise, were arranged on a friendly basis.

The Secretary's optimistic dream was to repeat last year's lists, but always there were adjustments to be made. Strong objections were raised to playing Netherton St Michael, since they had secured the services of that vicious demon bowler who had once or twice turned out for the county second eleven. Charlham were out, for we were still indignant about the capricious behaviour of their umpire (regardless of the fact that we ourselves had been known to claim that our own umpire was as good as a couple of extra men in the side any day!)

Someone proposed that West Hammerby be excluded, on the grounds that when visiting there last year we had had to eat our tea in a rather cramped chicken house. Our discomfort had been increased by a two-hour thunder-storm which had caused the match to be abandoned.

Sighing, the Secretary accepted these limitations. The post, by the way, was one of the few open to girls. Others were those of score-keeper and tea-ladies, though these were inferior tasks which did not warrant attendance at annual general meetings. It was taken for granted that wives, mothers, sisters, and girlfriends could always be relied on to rally round.

Theoretically the Secretary was on the selection committee, whose task was to meet once a week to choose the team for the next match. It was supposed to be his duty to notify those chosen, but in practice he seldom turned up, and so this was yet another job for the Captain. What was most likely to happen was that the Captain, at the end of a match, would say, 'Well, see you again next week.' And that was that.

The Treasurer's report naturally triggered off arguments about the usual problem of keeping going without raising the subscription rate which had stood at half-a-crown ever since the club had re-started in 1921. Why raise it now? Couldn't we think of a few more potential vice-presidents? Or arrange some whist-drives? Or stage a charity match on August Bank Holiday (no good if harvest happened to be early!)?

Any other business. Inevitably there would be some. Members were not giving up an evening away from their homes without using the opportunity for saying their piece. And inevitably there was the negative character, the eternal pessimist, to be dealt with.

So the AGM drew leisurely to its close. And the handful of us who normally did all the work knew that if we had sat around a home fireside, enjoying a drink, we could have settled everything in half-an-hour. But we always went through the routine. It was the proper way to do things.

The Chairman plodded through his agenda, the Secretary kept the minutes, and each resolution was properly proposed, seconded, and put to the meeting. Members addressed the chair instead of each other (unless the atmosphere became too heated!) Majority verdicts were accepted. Votes of thanks were duly passed.

And so, in a village hall, another generation received its training in the working of democracy. And still does, for from now to the end of March innumerable AGMs of local organisations will be in progress on each weekday evening. What a fortunate country we are, to possess such a tradition.

Shepherds are still a race apart

May 1983

It has been a good lambing season. The ewes came through the relatively mild winter in fine shape, and supplies of fodder held out well, so there was no question of short rations. Lowland farmers reckon that a lambing average of 165% is excellent, and this spring many of them have done better than that.

A neighbour of mine had not only a good proportion of twins and a number of triplets, but one of his ewes delivered quads. Naturally delighted, he planned a rewarding future for those four little lambs, but unhappily one of them had its throat slashed by a fox when it was about four days old. Most foxes will snap up a newly-born lamb straight from its mother's body if they have the chance, but for a fox to kill a lamb four days old is unusual.

The shepherd in this instance, a keen observer of wild life, tracked the fox to her lair and, with the help of two stalwart sons at a week-end dig, ensured that she would take no further toll of his flock. A neighbour who witnessed the act of retribution expressed strong disapproval, but her protests had little effect on the shepherd. That the fox would strike again was as certain as nightfall, and no shepherd could be expected to share a farm with a lamb-killing vixen.

Shepherds are a race apart from other farm-workers and always have been. Independent and autocratic, they have one priority in their lives - their sheep. My father was partly raised by his uncles, who were shepherds on Salisbury Plain getting on for a hundred years ago.

He once heard a farmer say of Jesse, one of the uncles, 'Ah well, I can't put it off any longer. I allow I shall have to go up to the sheepfold and see

Jesse. But, to tell the truth, I'd as soon stand in a field and let somebody blaze away at me with a double-barrelled gun as to go and talk with that cantankerous old sod!'

The reason was that he had to break to the shepherd the news that the hay supply was running low and that the sheep would have to go on short rations.

A G Street used to tell a similar story of a shepherd who gave notice because his employer had sold a hay-rick without consulting him. No, he agreed that the sheep didn't exactly need it, but the principle was wrong. He was shepherd, and he expected to be consulted before a decision was taken on any matter which might concern the sheep. If I remember rightly, he got an apology, and the deal for the sale of the hay-rick was cancelled. That, at least, is the probable end of the story.

The shepherd's life was one of solitude. Not of loneliness, for he had the sheep for company, but the sort of solitude which gives a man ample time to think. At lambing-time he was even divorced from his wife and family for six weeks, living in an austere little hut on the edge of the sheep-fold and rising every two hours or so, day and night, to tend newly-born lambs. On the great arable farms which were once characteristic of much of England the flock spent much of the year being folded on crops such as turnips and clover, but in late summer they spent a two-months' holiday on the open downs which lay beyond the fenced fields of the farms.

There for a time the shepherd really did enjoy the kind of pastoral idyll which romantic poets attributed to him. He lay on his back and gazed dreamily at the white clouds sailing overhead. He worked patiently with his knife at homely craft artefacts for sale at the autumn fairs. Decorated throwing-sticks were a favourite object.

I have seen such sticks, like small clubs two or three feet long, carved from end to end with scenes which have caught the shepherd's fancy. One depicted a fox hunt, with hounds in full cry after the fox and with accessories such as the huntsman's horn and ship and a hand holding a brimming glass of ale. On another the shepherd had carved pictures of his own tools - his crook, his bells, a hurdle and the pocket-knife he was using.

He also fashioned yokes for suspending bells around the sheep's necks, and pegs to fasten them. A thin wand of dry yew-wood I was once shown had been carved from end to end with arrow-shaped pegs, which could be snapped off one by one as needed. Carving dry yew-wood with a pocket-knife must have been an arduous and lengthy operation.

While he worked he listened to the music of the bells. Every flock of sheep was equipped with them. For a flock of two or three hundred sheep there might be a dozen or twenty bells, fastened to the necks of the leaders of the flock. The shepherd was well aware of which individuals those were. In a flock of that size he knew every sheep.

When the sheep were quietly grazing he would hear the occasional gentle tinkling, as the animals moved slowly over the sward, nibbling at the short turf. Sometimes a rhythmic swinging told him that the flock was on the march, probably on the way to the pond for a drink, but worth investigation. Sometimes an inharmonious jangling warned of trouble: the sheep were alarmed and in full flight. It sent the shepherd in haste to see what was amiss.

Sheep-bells, incidentally, are by no means obsolete. I have a collection of them which I used regularly till my farming days ended in the late 1960s. Most of them were made by specialist metal-smiths, though some shepherds used makeshift bells consisting of iron bolts suspended in old tins.

Some shepherds used the days of solitude for deep meditation. That the story of David Saunders, *The Shepherd of Salisbury Plain,* should have been a favourite religious tract of Victorian times was apt enough. Not a few shepherds became powerful non-conformist preachers, tramping many miles over the downs to take services in village chapels. I remember one such, Shepherd Keel, who was a joy to listen to.

Not that a shepherd could commit himself to many fixed engagements, the sheep always taking priority. An old book of the early nineteenth century, which I greatly treasure, tells of an old shepherd who felt the need to apologise for his non-attendance at church services. He evidently belonged to the tradition which decreed that a shepherd should be buried with a tuft of wool on his breast, enabling St Peter to identify him as a shepherd and so forgive him his sins of omission.

This old shepherd said that when once he did manage to get to church the parson described a wonderful place called Paradise. It sounded a most attractive location, said the old chap, and he thought he might like to go there. Then, he said, 'I got to thinking about it some more, and it come to me that if only there were a trout stream in Longcombe Bottom, where I do keep the sheep every now and then, I'd as soon be there as in Paradise.'

Happy fellow! He had learned the secret of making his own Paradise in the place he knew best.

On cats

July 1984

Most bird and beast corpses that I pick up find their way to the dissecting table of a veterinary naturalist who, in due course, supplies me with information, often surprising, about cause of death. One recent post-mortem verdict that occasioned no surprise featured a greenfinch I had found in my garden.

'Your greenfinch was definitely killed by a medium-sized or small mammal,' my friend reported. 'It was bitten through the skull and through the neck. The most likely candidate is a cat, once again, and to judge from the size and position of the teeth-marks I would say that the predator wasn't very large. Do you have a smallish cat visiting the garden?'

My immediate reply was that I don't. The cats in my neighbours' houses are both large ones, and I have never seen any other trespassing on my property. And then I thought. What do I know about what cats visit my garden? The place could be familiar territory to a dozen cats without my being any the wiser. What does anyone know about the behaviour of any individual cat?

One of the first cats I remember was a lethargic old marmalade cat who shared a cottage with a retired farm worker. It spent much of the day sleeping on his lap.

'Never goes farther than the end of the garden,' the old chap declared. 'I puts en out last thing at night, and first thing in the morning, there he is on the doorstop, waiting to be let in.' Except for one morning, when he failed to appear. Later that day he was released from a rabbit snare, a good two miles from home.

On the farm when I was a boy we had a dynasty of cats descended from a crippled tortoiseshell female we had found in an outlying barn. One of her front paws was permanently deformed where it had set itself after having been released from a gin (prevalent everywhere in those days). The injury had not prevented her from producing and caring for a family of kittens, which were fat and lively when we found them.

I could well appreciate the authenticity of the portrait of the cat in that memorable book, *The Incredible Journey*. After spending months trekking homewards across the north Canadian wilderness the two dogs were in bad shape and only just able to stagger in, but the cat who was their companion was as sleek and well-fed as when he started out, and there was evidence that he had found energy to sire a family or two of kittens en route.

When my radio programme, *Cowleaze Farm*, was on the air I remember pointing out to the two schoolgirls on one of our country walks a tabby-cat sitting quietly in the bottom of a hedge. It was a cat they knew well, having often stroked and tickled it on the kitchen hearth-rug, but when they reached out hands to touch it, there in the hedge, they drew back, disconcerted.

'It doesn't look like Bim,' they said. 'It looks like a wild creature. It's got a wild look in its eyes.'

'That's all part of being a cat,' I assured them.

A volatile creature, a cat can change moods like a chameleon changes colour. It likewise learns quickly from experience and adapts accordingly.

A friend who lived in a woodland area in pre-myxomatosis days shared his establishment with two Jack Russell terriers and a cat. The terriers took their daily exercise in one of the several rabbit-infested hedgerows in the vicinity, first sending a bevy of rabbits scampering for their burrows and then undertaking the strenuous operation of digging them out. In true Jack Russell style, they worked up a fury like berserk Vikings, spattering the countryside with soil for yards around, tearing at obstructing roots, and uttering appropriate war-cries. The cat meantime stationed itself strategically on the quiet side of the hedge, waiting patiently for a refugee rabbit to pop out. My friend said that time and again he saw the cat sloping off with its reward, while the dogs continued their frenzied assault for half-an-hour or so after the operation was really over.

No friction existed between the cat and dogs. There never does beween cats and other animals sharing the same home (I use the word 'animals' in the sense of mammals; few cats can be trusted with a canary or budgerigar).

Once when we moved house we left behind a cat for our successors, thinking that she was too old to make the move. Dogs are primarily attached to people, but cats to places. The newcomers brought with them a dog – a quiet spaniel who had been brought up with cats and so had long ago overcome any antipathy he might have had towards them. The cat had also been used to sharing the home with dogs. So, after taking stock of each other warily for a couple of days, they settled down to a life apparently of tolerant indifference.

About a fortnight later a big pugnacious Boxer dog invaded the garden and pitched into the spaniel, who stood no chance against such a weighty adversary. The cat, indoors, heard the rumpus, went to the window and saw what was going on. With hardly a moment's hesitation she bounded, a fireball of spitting, bristling, sharp-clawed vengeance, and landed accurately on that Boxer's back.

The battle was over instantly. The Boxer vanished and never ventured into the garden again. And the spaniel's owners marvelled at the perspicacity of a cat who was prepared, on an instant, to go to the rescue of a dog she had known for only two weeks.

She was a tortoiseshell cat, being a female. All tortoiseshell cats are female and all gingers male; at least, that is an almost inviolable rule, though I suppose that someone will write to tell me of an exception. And many, though not all, white cats are deaf.

On the farm in my boyhood days spaying cats, of either sex, was unheard of. We simply disposed of the numerous surplus kittens. For some reason May kittens were supposed to be unlucky. One theory for this illogical belief was that as May kittens were half-grown by August and September, when adders were about, there was always a danger that they would bring snakes indoors. But I don't believe that was the real reason.

Of somewhat later date is the incident of two ginger cats, one male, the other spayed, which lived in adjoining houses and were sworn enemies. Neither would allow the other on its territory. But one day the spayed cat crept into its enemy's house and sat on the rug, and the rightful occupant took no notice. That night the old lady, with whom the spayed ginger had lived, died. Her cat never went back, but the two cats thereafter lived together quite amicably to the end of their days.

The more one thinks about that episode, the more uncanny it seems. The cat whose mistress was dying recognised the approach of death in the house before it came. And so, it appears, did the ginger male next door.

More on cats

February 1985

To judge from the volume of subsequent correspondence, one of the most popular subjects I can choose for these articles is Cats. The last time I wrote about them I received letters from readers in Indonesia, Trinidad, Zambia, West Germany and three places in England.

On that occasion I mentioned my belief, widely held, that almost all tortoiseshell cats are female and all ginger cats male. My Zambian correspondent assures me that this is not so and offers a lesson in genetics to prove it. 'The mechanism of inheritance operates in such a way that ginger females will result only from the mating of a tortoiseshell with a ginger tom,' she tells me. 'Thus, taking into account all the possible crosses involving the sex-linked black/orange gene, we have:

Ginger tom x black female;
Black tom x ginger female;
Black tom x tortoiseshell female;
Ginger tom x tortoiseshell female.

'The incidence of ginger females is about one in five, which is why we don't often come across them,' she adds. And she suggests that a possible union between two ginger cats would give all ginger progeny,- which I am inclined to doubt, for surely there could be one or two throw-backs?

And then she casts what could be a pinch of doubt on the whole argument by mentioning that she has made the acquaintance of only one or two ginger females in more than fifty years, although she has known and owned numerous ginger males. That tallies with my own experience. If one ginger cat in five is a female I wonder why we have not met more of them? And has anyone ever seen a tortoiseshell tom?

My West German correspondent advises me that behind the duck pond at Russells Water, a village in the Chilterns between Henley-on-Thames and Oxford, is an inn named The Beehive which has a matching pair of ginger females, of 1981 vintage. They were part of a crop of feral females in the district.

She sends an attractive picture of her descendants, but somewhere in the course of the somewhat involved genealogy I must have lost my way, for this is a photograph of a delightful *tortoiseshell* mother with seven healthy kittens. Two of these are ginger, and they, I am assured, are toms. There are also two grey and two black ones, and the sire is thought to be a grey male resident on a neighbouring farm. Evidently a ginger father isn't necessary to produce ginger male progeny.

Concerning my mention of a dynasty of cats which ruled our farm for many years after we had rescued their matriarch, a maimed tortoiseshell, from the wild, a letter from a reader in Sumatra recounts some of the hazards besetting cats in that tropical land. They have, he says, to dodge dogs, rats, iguanas, owls, hawks, pigs and other wild predators as well as take their chance with unsympathetic humans. Most cats there have deformed tails, some due to a fashion for breaking the tails at birth and some through a genetical defect which results in stump-tailed specimens, presumably like Manx cats.

He relates the story of a stump-tailed female who got caught up in the fan-belt of a jeep. Although badly mauled, she did not appear to be bleeding internally so my correspondent went off to track down a vet, giving instructions to a garden boy to keep an eye on her while he was away. On his return the lad said the cat had died and he had disposed of the body.

Five weeks later the cat turned up, in a pitiable condition, on the doorstep. The vet, who examined her with a minimum of delay, said she had suffered three broken paws, a broken rear knee and hind leg, a broken pelvis and numerous cuts and bruises, besides which she was almost dead from starvation. It seemed incredible that she could have survived, but she did, and all the fractures in due course healed well.

Local people, when questioned, admitted having seen her around for two or three weeks and said that she was always accompanied by another poor specimen, who, however, licked her constantly. The vet noted that all her wounds were clean, including those which she herself would have been unable to reach.

Stories such as this must be at the root of the tradition that cats have nine lives. And the loving care exhibited by the injured cat's companion is heart-warming.

On the deafness of white cats, two readers point out that the cats which are so afflicted always have blue eyes. White cats with green or yellow eyes generally have normal hearing. So has a white cat with one blue eye and one of another colour. I remember that my old friend, the late Brian Vesey-Fitzgerald, used also to maintain that the cat must be pure white. Even one or two coloured hairs, he asserted, will upset the correlation between its white colour and deafness.

It seems, too, that many deaf cats are also mute. As with humans, there seems to be a frequent association between deafness and dumbness. On the other hand, deaf cats are very sensitive to vibrations. Brian Vesey-Fitzgerald also added the curious observation that a deaf white cat will usually refuse to climb. Why that should be so I cannot suggest.

In the matter of vibrations, many cats show a fondness for walking on piano keys, presumably enjoying the vibrations. There have been instances of deaf cats learning to run along a piano keyboard in order to attract attention, having presumably noticed that such activity usually brought some human into the room, to see what was amiss.

Many observers, of whom Brian Vesey-Fitzgerald was one, were convinced that cats were aware of what we would call the supernatural. They could, he said, see ghosts and were not afraid of them.

Many years ago, in my father's time, there lived in our village, a born-again Christian with a gift of oratory but an argumentative temperament. Having fallen out with the Anglicans, the Methodists and the Baptists, he held revivalist meetings in his own house until, in due course, he was able to found his own mission hall. When on Sunday evenings his congregation used to assemble his cat remained curled up sleeping in her chair by the fire .... until he started to pray. Whereupon she shot up, bristling, and made for the door. Care was taken to leave the door ajar, for once or twice, when it was shut, she scrambled up the curtains, with resultant disaster to the windowsill geraniums, and once went up the chimney. The preacher swore that the devil was in that cat!

A boiling fowl for dinner

March 1986

One of my elderly neighbours hailed me as I walked down the street.

'Can you come and kill an old hen for me?'

'I expect so,' I agreed.

'Tis me rheumatics,' she explained. 'I han't got the strength in me wrists.'

So I did the job, and stayed to help her pluck it. Later in the day her daughter thanked me. 'I don't know why she bothers,' she added. 'She doesn't need to. Still, it's no good arguing with her, and I couldn't wring a chicken's neck to save my life. I can't understand how <u>you</u> can do it, you being so interested in birds.'

The old hen whose life I terminated was one of seven which have lived in my neighbour's back garden for the past four or five years. Twice a day she has fed them, calling and talking to them as she hobbled down the path to their pen. She knew each one individually, of course, and they knew her. Now this hen, the most aged of them, had come to the end of a laying period and had shed about half her feathers.

'Won't start laying again for months. I reckon I may as well have her for dinner.' And so she did.

I understood her attitude. She and I both belong to a generation and an environment that accepted such matters without question. Food was something which, as far as possible, we acquired ourselves, not purchased in a shop.

In my family household we drank milk and ate butter derived from our own cows, baked bread from our own wheat, grew our own vegetables, and boiled our hens when they became too old to provide us with eggs. Most villagers kept a pig which was treated much as a family pet, until the time came for it to be a November sacrifice and a main source of meat for the coming winter.

Long before my age had reached double figures I had seen cocks treading hens and bulls serving cows; I had seen calves and lambs born; and I had assisted my father in his duties as the unofficial village pig-killer. Rabbits shot by my father on Saturday afternoons comprised a high proportion of the fresh meat on our table. Birth and death were familiar events to me.

It was true that great sadness came to our house for a half-a-day when my father had to take old Gyp, the terrier who had shared our lives ever since I could remember, out to the yard and shoot her, but what else could he do when the poor old girl obviously had incurable cancer? Unpleasant duties such as this a man had to be prepared to undertake.

In the urban civilisation that overwhelmingly prevails at this end of the century we have erected a barrier between ourselves and the natural cycle of life and death. More animals and birds than ever before are bred, reared, and killed for us to eat, but we are shielded from the actual processes. We do not have to take the sow to boar, we do not have to stay up all night helping a cow with a difficult calving, we do not have to wring a fowl's neck and then pluck and disembowel her (at least, most of us don't, though, as noted, I have just done so!) And when, like my neighbour's daughter, we are confronted with one of these basic aspects of life, we tend to shudder and recoil.

Spring is on the wing. Already I have seen the first snowdrops and heard the first robins and thrushes singing. Hazel catkins are scattering their pollen all over the woods, and any day now I expect to see the first brimstone butterfly emerging from hibernation and flexing its wings. Soon these first tentative ventures of new life will merge into a stream, then a mighty river in full flood. There will be an upsurge of birth, new creatures being born everywhere.

And what will happen to them? Long before the autumn days start closing in, by far the greater proportion of them will be dead. It is necessary that that should happen. If all the progeny of a single pair of flies were to survive the summer they would amount to billions and vast areas of the earth would be uninhabitable for other species. But, of course, it is the role of flies to provide food for a multitude of other creatures.

For some insects, such as mayflies, life is so short that they do not, in their final imago stage, feed and have no mouth-parts or digestive organs. All they have to do is to dance for an hour or two in the spring sunshine, mate, lay their eggs and die.

The population of blue tits in Britain is relatively static, being estimated at around five million pairs. A pair of blue tits have only one brood in a summer, as a rule, but that brood usually consists of from five to twelve young ones. Let us put the average at eight. With father and mother that amounts to a family of ten. Yet if the population is to remain static, before the next breeding season eight of the family must die. If the parents survive, then all the juveniles must perish. Their death is a necessity.

It is not, however, necessarily a tragedy. It is only human sentiment that so regards it. The old hen whose neck I wrung had come to the end of her life, and I ensured that death came to her quickly and painlessly. She had had a much longer and pleasanter life than those supermarket chicken we eat, which spend their brief lives of about eleven weeks in a congested hothouse. They have this in common, however, with the vast majority of creatures about to be born this spring - they die long before they reach maturity.

But a life span is a matter of relativity. Life must seem as long to a mayfly enjoying its nuptial dance on a May afternoon as to a three-hundred-years-old oak falling to the woodman's axe. And the end is the same.

I refuse to accept that this is a morbid theme. When first I visited America, years ago, I commented that four subjects generally taboo at meal-times in Britain, were freely discussed over there. They were sex, religion, the workings of the speaker's stomach, and how much money he or she possessed.

The range of table conversation has since been somewhat extended over here, but there is still a reluctance in both countries to discuss death. In this respect our immediate ancestors were more open and uninhibited than we are. Perhaps because they encountered death so much more frequently than we do.

Death is necessary and inevitable, and to keep alive Man must deal it out. All that is required of him is that when he is the killer he should be merciful. And my own view, perhaps a minority one, is that he should kill only from necessity, not for pleasure or recreation.

Comfort has its price

April 1986

Do not be put off by the apparent frivolity of my opening anecdote. It is leading in the right direction.

It comes from a small book, *The Specialist*, only 29 pages, which had a tremendous vogue some 50 years ago, running through about 30 printings. It purports to be the reminiscences of an American back-woods carpenter in pioneering days who had the initiative to specialise. And what he chose to specialise in was the construction of those outdoor privies which were once such an essential feature of cottage life in Britain as well as America. A client once came to him with a complaint about a privy he had built up, so Lem went along to see what the trouble was. It was right in the middle of haymaking. Hiding behind a barn, he watched the hired men visiting the little house and noted that they stayed there for an hour. Investigating further, he concluded that he had made 'them holes too durn comfortable. So I gets out a scroll saw and cuts 'em square, with hard edges.'

He went back to his observation post and exclaimed triumphantly: 'I watched them hired hands goin' in and out, and not one of them was stayin' more than four minutes!'

The first motor vehicle acquired by our family was a one-ton Ford van, which my father, a peasant-farmer of the old school, bought in 1921. Up to that time the farm produce round, which he ran in the nearest market town, had been serviced by a pony and trap. Our new transport came from an Army surplus sale and, having been intended for use in France, had a left-hand drive.

Very proud we were when it was delivered, painted bright green with my father's name inscribed in yellow letters on both sides. It did not take long to equip it for its new career. A long cushion stuffed with horsehair was laid on the board seat behind the steering-wheel. Behind it the men fixed up a rail as a back-rest, and behind that was a shelf for boxes of eggs, cans of milks or crates of poultry.

More durable commodities, such as cabbages, sacks of potatoes, logs and peasticks, sat on the floor. Peasticks, beansticks and clothes-posts often protruded from the back, making it necessary to tie the rear doors half-open. There were no regulations in those days against ladling milk out of a bucket in a vehicle loaded with miscellaneous produce.

Driving the van was a two-man operation. The driver needed a mate sitting by his side to look out and put his hand out when a right turn loomed. It was too far from the driver to stretch across the width of the van and stick out his own hand, nor could he see what was approaching from the rear. There were, of course, no automatic signals.

The steering column sprang, almost upright, from the floorboards. Beneath the steering-wheel were two levers, one on either side. One controlled the sparking rate, which needed apparently frequent adjustment; the other was the accelerator. There were no gears!

Eh? No gears? Well, there were two foot pedals, of which one was the foot-brake. The other was officially the clutch, combined with low gear. When the van had to go uphill and started to labour, the driver pressed his foot on this pedal and kept it there! Until the top of the hill was reached and the vehicle could move into top gear again. When climbing a long hill the engine became very hot. You could glance down at a gap in the floor-boards, near the foot-pedals, and see the exhaust-pipe glowing red-hot. I cannot remember ever feeling apprehensive about the van catching fire, though the heat penetrated through the soles of my boots.

In those days no regulations existed restricting the uses to which a vehicle could be put. So having pressed the van into use for all manner of farm jobs, during the week my father would occasionally take the family out for an outing. It was brushed out and equipped with wooden benches, arranged length-wise, and my mother and aunt provided themselves with cushions. The back doors were propped open, so that we could enjoy a little of the scenery, and away we went, bound for a picnic. I treasure a photo of the whole family spreading the picnic hampers and cloths over the stones of Stonehenge.

What impresses me most as I look back on our trips in the old van is the lack of comfort. One could hardly be comfortable sitting bolt upright on a hard seat while striving hard to maintain the pressure on a pedal growing hot enough for a blacksmith to work on. To say nothing of the shuddering jolts every few yards as the vehicle bumped over pot-holes or skidded in ruts. And it wasn't much easier for the passengers, swaying and falling against each other in the back. I have known times when it was a positive relief to have to clamber out and push the boiling vehicle up a sharp hill.

By contrast, motoring today is ultra-comfortable. We sit in luxuriously upholstered armchairs, radio providing background music, simple buttons and switches offering every control we need, even gear changes if we have an automatic model. It is so soothing and relaxing that we tend to forget we are hurtling along at 70 miles per hour .... until we need to come to a sudden stop.

Which thought brings us back to Lem, the specialist, and his privy. Would his solution to his problem work with cars, do you think? If cars were less comfortable, would there be fewer accidents?

It would not be necessary to return to the primitive discomforts of our old Ford van. Something rather more sophisticated is indicated. For instance, a moderately painful electric shock when the speed limit was exceeded!

It may sound ludicrous, much as Lem's seats with square edges, but the carnage on the roads, mainly through unwise speeding, is not laughable.

The wood for the job

February 1985

The farmer and I stood surveying the wreckage. A careless tractor-driver had backed against an old chalk-cob wall and caused a section to collapse into the farmyard.

'A pity,' said the farmer, ruefully. 'I suppose we shall have to repair it with concrete blocks. Nobody knows how to build chalk-cob nowadays.'

He was wrong there. I do, but I refrained from telling him so. The days when I was willing to volunteer for hard manual work are past.

He ran his hand along one of the timbers to which the thatched roof of the wall had been fixed, though sticking out of the debris at awkward angles, not one of them was broken. 'Sound as a bell,' he commented. 'And I bet they've been there well over a hundred years. I wonder what wood it is?'

I could tell him that, too. 'That be abele,' I said, and I pronounced it 'abeel', just as the old chap had who originally introduced me to this timber. I could hear the old man's voice again, see his portly figure sitting, legs wide apart, in the old wicker armchair by the glowing fire of his workshop.

'Uncle Isaac', we called him, but I think he was my father's third or fourth cousin or something like that. All his life he had been a woodman, of a special sort. He used to buy small standing timber in the numerous woods and coppices around our village, fell it, and transport it back to his workshop for fashioning into a variety of interesting articles.

He could, if required, weave wattle hurdles, but any competent underwood craftsman could do that in the woods, without having recourse to a workshop, so Uncle Isaac tended towards articles that needed more sophisticated tools, most of which he himself had made. He had pole-lathes, spoke-shaves mounted on frames, bow-saws, cleaving knives, froes, vices, bond-splitters and an assortment of what he called 'engines', which appeared to me to be various hand-made types of wooden planes.

His workshop was an old cottage at the end of the yard behind his house. An iron-barred open fireplace had been installed in the chimney corner, and there a fire, replenished with waste chogs of wood, burned day and night throughouit the winter. In summer when the fire was out, you could climb over the fireplace and, looking up, see the sky at the top end of the chimney. There were two almost shapeless wicker armchairs, equipped with dirty cushions, one on either side of the fireplace. One was occupied by Uncle Isaac, the other by a black-and-white cat. In winter I never saw the cat's chair vacant.

As a boy on the farm, I used to envy Uncle Isaac and his cat. After having spent days threshing or dung-spurling or carting mangolds or picking sprouts, I felt I was in the wrong job. I would far rather be a craftsman in wood, making interesting things with that fascinating array of tools in the cosy workshop on wet and icy days. And Uncle Isaac had the best of both worlds, for in summer you would find him outside in the yard, making or painting ladders, mending hay-rakes and doing those jobs which required more space than the interior of the cottage.

But every man to his father's profession, and my father was a farmer. So the most I could do was to escape to Uncle Isaac's workshop on wet afternoons when I would not be missed on the farm. I used to pester him to be allowed to use his tools, and I think it pleased the old man (then in his eighties) to have a youngster around as an audience. That was how I came to know about abele.

'That be abele', he had said, when I asked him about a round, white pole in a corner of the workshop. 'You do use that for rafters for the thatch capping on the tops of mud-walls. Always abele. Nothin' else will do.'

Well, that isn't quite so. Since then I have seen other kinds of timber used for the purpose, though perhaps for repair jobs by builders unfamiliar with the old lore. But Uncle Isaac was a stickler for tradition.

For every job of which he was the master there was a type of timber better suited to it than any other.

I suppose the rules were based on generations of experience, so doubtless abele (better known as white poplar) has qualities which fit it ideally for use in roofing cob walls, though what they are I don't know, and I suppose that now nobody cares. At a guess I would say that it is because poplar is light, long-lasting, and very resistant to fire. It was formerly used, too, for the floors of oast-houses, where hops were dried.

My encounter with abele, after all these years, brought back to mind some other examples of Uncle Isaac's timber lore. Apart from hazel, which was employed for weaving wattle-hurdles, making eel-traps and cleaving for spar-gads, ash, oak and elm were his favourite woods.

Elm he used for the seats of three-legged milking stools (of which he made large quantities). Also for the massive hubs of waggon wheels; for pig-killing stools; for troughs for mixing dough; for wedges; and for the seats of chairs, for tables and for stair treads. Elm is very resistant to water, and, having a twisted grain, doesn't easily split.

Ash for the sides (poles) of ladders; for the shafts and undercarriages of waggons; for yokes for carrying buckets (this too was one of Uncle Isaac's specialities); for the straight sides of sheep cribs; for the legs of milking stools; and for steaming and kneading into shape the sinuous handles of scythes ('sneeds' they were called).

Uncle Isaac had access to no great quantity of oak, the mighty trunks being in demand for building, but he liked to have a reasonable stock in hand for ladder rungs and wheel spokes. When he could get them he cleft lengths of oak saplings to make oak fencing stakes, and he normally had a stock of cylindrical oak pegs, as substitutes for nails. He always had an eye for an oak branch whose shape suggested that it would be useful as a support strut for an angle in a timber-framed building, and he liked to obtain some of the root wood for cutting into sections for tool handles.

The less common woods also had their places in Uncle Isaac's almanac. Sycamore was for making butterpats and butter beaters. Also for the rollers in mangles and for the kitchen table-tops which in those days conscientious housewives would scrub until they were glistening white.

Birch saplings of the right size were cut and bundled up for despatch to the New Forest, where a besom-making industry flourished. The brake-blocks of waggons, for use on iron-rimmed wheels, were usually of willow. In the annex where he fashioned sneads, Uncle Isaac generally had a supply of blackthorn saplings being transformed into knobbly walking-sticks, and also of hazel rods with a fork in the proper place to be made into thumb-sticks. Lime wood was set aside for the local cobblers and saddlers, for cutting blocks.

Uncle Isaac's workshop failed to survive long enough to be converted into a 'period residence'. Its foundations lie under a modern housing estate. His hand-made tools and equipment doubtless perished by fire long ago. The age-old lore of his craft lingers only in the memories of the spectators such as myself, for of what practical use is it now to know that holly wood makes the best 'swingers' for flails? Or that the proper wood for rafters on the top of cob walls is 'abele'?

Roots of the family tree – and the topic of Capricorn

March 1984

The intercontinental planes that perform the beneficent service of carrying *The Guardian Weekly* to Papua, Paraguay, Peking, Pietermaritzburg and many other remote parts, apparently take on as cargo for the return journey innumerable sacks of mail, of which I get my fair share.

And at least half the letters I receive from overseas are from exiles from England (though many of them are several generations removed) who are eager to trace their roots in the 'homeland'. Usually their researches are well advanced and they are requiring details of some worthy blacksmith, butcher, beer retailer, or higgler (now there's a lovely name for an occupation! - I think he was a small-time peripatetic trader) who lived in a country parish a hundred or two years ago.

Genealogy as a study for amateurs steadily increases in popularity. To aid the growing army of ancestor seekers, family history societies have been formed in most counties or divisions of counties, and associations of those who share the same surname multiply. There is even a Whitlock Genealogical Research Group, which issues an occasional Whitlock Family Newsletter, though I regret that I have not found time to be a particularly active member.

I have, however, done my share of digging in parish registers - an exercise which now generally involves a visit to the county archives, though some registers are still kept under lock and key by the parish incumbent. They tend to be reasonably comprehensive back to the beginning of the nineteenth century, though with some gaps, but earlier than that they become progressively patchier.

It is worth remembering that what the registers record are baptisms, marriages, and funerals at the parish church, not births, marriages, and deaths in the parish, and there *is* a difference. Dissenters and persons of other religions may, for instance, find no place in the parish registers. Much also depends on the characters of successive parish clerks. Some kept their records conscientiously, making their entries in copper-plate script, while others merited the sack with ignominy.

Even when they did their best the material they had to deal with was complicated and confusing to us of a different generation. The sedentary habits of our ancestors tended to produce communities of which the members were almost inextricably related.

For instance, in my native parish in the middle of the Victorian era out of about 300 inhabitants nearly 100 bore my surname. Among them were two young men named George Whitlock, each married to a wife named Elizabeth, producing their families at the same time. So when the register records the baptism of a child whose parents were George and

Elizabeth there is nothing to indicate which pair of parents the entry refers to.

No doubt it was perfectly plain to their contemporaries, who probably had distinguishing nicknames for them, but the diligent parish clerk who recorded the baptism was concerned with observing the law, not with posterity. So we grope and conjecture.

Perhaps the most useful of all aids to the study of parish registers and the unravelling of a family tree is the 1851 census. This comprehensive document records the population of each parish as the census officer found it on a March day in that year. The details recorded are the names of each person residing in each house, their relationship to the head of the family, their 'condition' (*ie* married, single or widowed), their age, their rank, profession or occupation and their place of birth.

No earlier census provided such a wealth of information. Moreover, the date is exactly right to be of the maximum use. Many of the younger individuals mentioned in the census lived on till within living memory, so providing a path deep into the past.

For instance, here on the first page is my great-grandfather William, who is a widower aged 35, living with his son aged nine and two daughters, aged five and three, and a twenty-eight-year-old niece as a housekeeper. Later in the census we discover a widow lady, aged 52, with a daughter aged 18 who is classified as a school-teacher, no doubt at a local dame's school.

We know, though *they* could have had no inkling of the course of events on that March morning of 1851, that William was destined to marry that eighteen-year-old girl and that much family friction would result.

Here too is my great-uncle Arthur, aged seven months, who, twelve years later, was widely blamed for setting fire to a barn and so starting a conflagration which burned down half the village. We who pore over the records and try to visualise the village as it was on that March day have a queer sense of feeling like God! Observing these good people going about their daily business we can say, 'Ah, you don't know what is going to happen to you, but we do!'

The quest for ancestors can lead into some strange corners and produce some unanticipated and perhaps unwelcome discoveries. The dedicated family genealogist should be prepared for an ancestor or two who ended their careers at the end of a hempen rope.

Searchers who hope to establish their descent from some distinguished person or some family run the risk of grave disappointment, as happened to an optimistic lady who once wrote to me, mentioning her 'pride of family'.

The family had an unusual surname. We will call it Capricorn, though it was something different. By diligent research she had traced her line back to a prosperous linen-draper in Bristol around the middle of the nineteenth century. There she was stuck, but, hovering tantalisingly just out of reach, was an Admiral Capricorn, who had had a distinguished career in the French wars. That was the sort of ancestor she wanted.

The truth of the matter, when she discovered it, was far different. The Admiral was so distinguished that he had had a ship of the line named after him. Nine months before the birth of the baby boy who was to become the prosperous linen-draper, *The Admiral Capricorn* put in at Bristol, and the sailors enjoyed their shore leave in the dockside taverns as sailors traditionally did.

When one of their entertainers, Annie Bundles, found herself pregnant she had no idea which sailor was the father of the coming baby. All she knew was that he belonged to *The Admiral Capricorn*. So, realising that about the only thing she could give her son was a good name, and not much liking the sound of Billy Bundles, she called him William Capricorn.

The glory of an English spring

May 1987

Not for several decades have we in England experienced such a spring as this. From the time of a weekend of gales and the following weekend of torrential rain, both in the first half of April, this notoriously fickle season had not put a foot wrong until last weekend when it was back to winter, with snow on the northern hills, hail, rain and winds.

So many poetic fancies about the idyllic delights of an English spring are confounded by the harsh realities; indeed if one took the first half of last month as a guide, Browning was wise to be in a warmer clime when he wrote, 'Oh, to be in England, now that April's there.'

The only phrase which seems to cover the situation is 'We don't have a climate - just weather.'

But for a fortnight or more it was glorious - and on such days, if I rise before dawn, as I often do, and wade forth happily into a world saturated in dew, by the time of the mid-day meal I am so tired that immediately afterwards I fall asleep. That way I waste an hour or so of the most brilliant sunshine of the day - the ideal hours for seeking spring butterflies. But if I manage to defy nature and deny myself a post-prandial nap, I am then so sleepy by nightfall that I cannot walk in the dusky woods to listen for nightingales and nightjars.

My problem, you see, is that, unlike some of those super-characters we hear about, I cannot make do on three or four hours' sleep. It is, in fact, the only reason I can think of, offhand, why I have missed being made Prime Minister.

Good intentions stand the best chance of being realised when they formulate themselves in the first hours of the day, before the frittering trivialities of everyday life have a chance to submerge them. May dew, as any old countryman, or rather, countrywoman, will tell you, is magic.

The fair maid who, on the first of May,
Goes to the fields at the break of day,
And washes in dew from the hawthorn tree,
Will ever after handsome be.

My long-deceased great-grandmother used to collect May dew in bottles, for use later in anointing her freckles, though why she wanted to get rid of the beautiful dappling of freckles is more than I can fathom. She also recalled seeing a sickly child drawn, naked, through grass wet with dew on three consecutive mornings, May 1st, 2nd and 3rd. We must hope that they chose a meadow free from thistles and nettles.

Perhaps the most effective contribution that May dew can make to our well-being is to coax us into the open air at daybreak. In that respect it is on a par with the maxim that 'an apple a day keeps the doctor away.' A doctor, on being asked his opinion of the saying, confirmed that it was accurate enough but added, 'provided you eat it, sitting on horseback, three miles from home, watching the sunrise!' Think it over.

I still have freckles (or are they the blotches of brown pigment that come with age?), but it is not for any effect that May dew may have on them that I like to dip my hands in it and rub it on my face. No, it is simply that I like the lovely refreshing sensation. And while I am enjoying it I can listen to the birds' dawn chorus.

In one week, towards the end of April, I heard on my morning walks the first chiffchaffs, willow-warblers, blackcaps, garden warblers, grasshopper warblers, cuckoos, tree-pipits, and nightingales. When these energetic migrants joined the choir of blackbirds, song-thrushes, robins, collared doves, chaffinches, greenfinches, starlings, wrens, hedge-sparrows and great tits, the effect was overwhelming. A glorious cascade of song. I took off my hat.

As though the ecstasy of sound were not enough, there was equal enchantment for the eyes. Every day now I note new flowers opening, and not just in ones and twos, as if tentatively testing the weather, but in sudden profusion. It seemed that every dainty birch tree in the entire forest decided to unfurl its catkins on the same morning.

For weeks primroses reigned supreme along the edge of woodland rides and in the clearings; then, suddenly, they were sharing the honours with wood anemones and were being challenged by bluebells. Already I can detect the leaves and flower stalks of the summer crop of orchids venturing into the sunlight.

Of the butterflies that appear in springtime almost all are hibernators. They survive the winter in the adult stage, emerging at the signal given by the increasing warmth of the sun. Without much expectation of seeing anything, we started our weekly patrols of a set two-mile route, recording butterflies for a Nature Conservancy survey, in the first weekend of April. To our surprise, we saw eleven on the first weekend; then a dud; and then scores of 19 and 26.

Most of them were brimstones, looking for all the world like primroses taking wing, but we saw also fair numbers of peacocks, small tortoiseshells and commas and one or two large and small whites. Any day now we hope to spot holly blues, then some of the fritillaries and, crowding in soon afterwards, all the superb insects of the summer woodlands.

When I miss the afternoon butterflies and seek compensation in what the evening twilight has to offer, I enjoy a bird chorus little inferior to the dawn song. Nightingales, though unpredictable, are most likely to sing in the late evenings, and if, as we hope, we wish to take a forest census of them, we have only six weeks for it. Once the cares of feeding a brood start to press in on it, the nightingale has no time for singing.

A bonus on my crepuscular rambles is the sight of woodcock roding, patrolling on flapping wings at tree-top height along the edge of clearings. And nightjars continue whirring like alarm clocks after the twilight has faded.

One of my daughters, embarking on a continental holiday, complains about delays through fog and through strikes at airports and about jostling crowds and ant-hill conditions almost everywhere. Even under the best travel conditions, I couldn't bear to leave England in springtime. I would be missing far too much.

Making the language ackle

March 1986

My great-grandfather William, whom I meet from time to time under the old apple-tree where he used to set up his cider-press, eyed my sparse covering of grey hair and commented, 'Ha, I see you be gettin' thin on top, like the rest of us! There, time ketches up wi' us all. Still, I suppose you can still lend a hand wi' the hilin', come harvest?'

'Yes, I dare say,' I replied, after a pause for consideration. It seemed simpler to agree than to try to explain to him that there was no hiling to be done, for the reason that modern harvesting produces no sheaves to be hiled.

That same afternoon, my thoughts running along memories of harvesting as I used to know it, I happened to mention hiling in the presence of my grandchildren, who enquired, 'What's hiling, Grandad?' It was no use referring them to my dictionary, for hiling isn't mentioned there. I checked on stooking, which is or was a synonym for the same operation in certain other regions of England, and that wasn't there, either.

Eventually I found a reasonably accurate definition under a specialised meaning of 'shock'. 'To shock - to arrange corn in shocks; shock - a group usually of twelve corn-sheaves stood up close together in field', said this dictionary. So, while the current editions of dictionaries survive, assiduous students of future generations will be able to check up on certain details of old-time harvesting, probably as familiar to Roman and Saxon farmers as to me but now sinking into obsolescence.

But hiling, as a word, will be lost, that seems sure. Dialect abounds in intriguing adjectives and nouns that describe forgotten objects, but verbs are even more fascinating, referring as they do to people in action. How many times have I heard my father issue the command, 'You, and you, and you go and hile ten-acres.' And, of course, we didn't need any further details of what we were expected to do.

At haymaking he might have said, 'Go and pook the hay.' Or, when the sheaves were being carted to the rick at harvest-time, he might tell me, 'You'd better pitch,' meaning that my job was to lift the sheaves by a two-grained prong and place them on the waggon. Later, when the summer's accumulation of farmyard manure was waiting to be spread over the fields his decision would be, 'Today we'll go spurling that dung.' We did that, incidentally, with four-grained prongs rather than two-grained. Goodness knows how many years ago it was that last I saw a man dung-spurling.

Some dialect words refer to even more specialised techniques. A hedger 'spleeshed' the bushes he used in his living hedge, that is, he cut each stem half-through just above ground level with his billhook. That enabled him to bend, and twist, and weave them as he would. After harvest it was time to 'wim' the seed corn. 'Wim' is another word for 'winnow', which again is an almost obsolete operation, certainly not one normally carried out on a farm.

Often I have heard my mother say, on her way out to the garden with her trug-basket, 'Well, I must go and shriggle those peas.' 'To shriggle' means to gather the last fruits of a crop. You can shriggle strawberries, apples, blackberries and other fruits, but not grain. The stray ears of corn were 'gleaned' not 'shriggled', by the widows and the poor of the parish. But in my district we didn't use even that word; we called it 'leazing'.

Ploughmen had their own technical words. When they came to the end of a 'rudge' (a land measurement for ploughing) they 'hinted' the last furrow, which meant they turned it over. When they started a new rudge they 'struck out' a furrow. The horses well understood the ploughman's language. They knew that 'Wug off' meant 'Turn to the right,' and 'Coom hidder' meant turn to the left. 'Hoist up, there,' urged them to get a move on, though its derivation is 'High step, there. ' If a horse stumbled it was said 'to lumper'. A useful, multi-purpose verb was 'to ackle'. How many times, in the years during and just after the war when new machinery was being introduced to the farm at an unprecedented pace, have I heard a farm worker lament, 'I can't get this yer contraption to ackle, not nohow!'? Mind you, his frustration didn't last long. A more versatile and adaptable generation of men never existed. They soon had the unfamiliar bit of hardware 'ackling', or functioning properly.

The rejection of many dialect words has been a loss to the language. A hen 'cackles' and a cock 'crows', but they utter other sounds as well, according to their various activities, and the observant countryman had words for them. A hen, calling her chicken,'checkles'. And what a lovely and descriptive verb Chaucer uses concerning the widow's cock Chauntecleer:

He chukketh, when he hath a corn i-founde
And to him renner than his wives alle.

A cock scratching in a dunghill and 'chukking' to call his wives when he discovered a titbit was once a familiar sight in every farmyard, and I remember often using Chaucer's word.

Instead of 'to empty' we used two words, 'to empt' and 'to unempt'. 'Empt' was used of liquids, 'unempt' of solids. You 'empted' a bucket of water but you 'unempted' a load of sheaves. An interesting distinction.

Then there are the verbs 'to prise' and 'to brise'. 'To prise', often spelt with a 'z', means to force open by leverage, but I have never been able to find in any standard dictionary its opposite 'to brise', meaning to press down hard, so as to seal (a lid, for instance). Yet it is a useful word, with no obvious alternative.

There are, though, instances of new uses being found for old words. As a boy I was more than once banished from a room where my mother was writing a letter.

'Go away! You're juddering me!'

But sometimes, when I was resting my hands on the table and jumping up and down, she would say, 'Stop it! You're making the table judder.'

A good old dialect word, I thought, and one whose passing was to be regretted. But then one day, I suppose it must have been in the 1950s, for recordings were made on discs rather than tape, I was in a BBC recording studio and was asked to repeat my performance. The producer explained, 'I'm sorry, but the apparatus was juddering!'

For her it wasn't a dialect word but a technical verb that fitted the situation exactly.

The passing bell and others

January 1984

After a programme of handbell ringing I enjoyed recently I was told by one of the ringers that when a ringer dies handbells are rung over the open grave. I gathered that, although this was a known tradition, it was one of which he himself had no first-hand knowledge, so perhaps it is on the edge of extinction.

The handbell ringing which gave rise to the conversation was an item in a Christmas concert, appropriately enough, for in times past both Christmas and the New Year were recognised festivals to be welcomed with bell music. Before the war, if I am not mistaken, the bells of St Paul's in London were rung at every quarter-hour until midnight on New Year's Eve, culminating in a full peal at midnight, to the delight of the Scottish revellers on the steps below. Thereafter the bells were silent, even if the Scots were not.

Another bell which is also silent now, probably a casualty of the war, was the Passing Bell. The last occasion I heard it must have been in 1938 or 1939. I was dung-spurling in a field about half-a-mile from the village when the sombre tolling began. A mournful stroke echoed across the valley, followed a minute or two later by another, and so on for an hour or more.

'That'll be old Albert passed on,' said my companion, though he was wrong. It was someone we wouldn't have thought of. We took off our caps and stood quiet and self-conscious for a few moments. The bell-ringer was a retired farmer who happened to live near the church and, because he liked to see the old customs kept up, substituted for the sexton, who was away at work all day.

Bell-ringing was prohibited during the war, except as a warning of enemy invasion, and by the war's end our bell-ringer had died. So the custom lapsed for lack of a successor. That must have been the sequence of events in many parishes.

Some bell-ringers would make their bells provide further details of the deceased. Three strokes for a man, two for a woman, one for a child. Other ringers muffled their bells for the death knell.

The 67th Canon of the Church of England, which, as far as I know, has never been rescinded, decrees: 'That when any is passing out of this life, a bell shall be tolled, and then the minister shall not then be slack to do his last duty.' The implication is that the bell should be tolled before the patient died, and that seems to have been the custom until at least the eighteenth century.

The sexton was the more assiduous in his duties because he was paid a set fee for tolling the passing bell - with double pay if he had to do it at night. The Canon suggests that the sexton was expected to be better informed about the course of events than the minister, whom he summoned by tolling the bell.

That indeed is the logical interpretation, for the message of bells has always been one of summons or warning. 'Look out!' 'Pay attention!' 'Achtung!' In medieval monasteries and on board ship bells marked the passing of the hours. The curfew bell told citizens that it was time to cover their fires and go to bed. The clanging bell of the fire engine served to warn the populace of fire, before it was replaced by the penetrating wail of the siren. My bicycle bell used to warn apparently sleep-walking pedestrians.

The ringing of bells to summon the faithful to church is a tradition that goes back at least to the Celtic missionaries who, in the Dark Ages, carried a bell on their enterprising journeys.

I was introduced to evidence of similar behaviour in, of all unlikely places, southern California. There the course of the Royal Road, trodden by Spanish monks four hundred years ago, is marked by bells attached to little frames. Every spring a party of these missionary monks would leave their Mexican base and tramp northwards along the coast to San Francisco. It was a leisurely progression. At every stage the ringing of a bell summoned the local Indians to gather for baptism, marriages, instruction in the faith and such healing as the monks were capable of. In autumn they returned south by similar easy stages.

A modern instance is a church I know in a remote district of Kenya. It is rightly termed a church, though it is simply an open space under a giant tree. The furniture consists of a reading desk, a small rickety table and some logs for use as seats. The steel rim of a lorry wheel hangs by a rope from a branch, and nearby an iron bar for beating it is kept. The sound is a passable reproduction of that of a church bell, and it serves the same purpose. Struck for twenty minutes or so before the service is due, it can usually by relied upon to summon a sizeable congregation.

The same bell can convey slightly different messages to different hearers. For instance, a set of sheep bells I have were once used to inform the shepherd about the movements of his flock when grazing on open downland.

I last used one of them in the late 1960s after, one Sunday afternoon, I had been caught unawares in the middle of a meadow by Oscar, an aggressive ram who was under the impression that he owned the farm. Thereafter intended victims always had due warning of his approach, and a more frustrated ram would have been hard to find. But his harem of ewes loved it. They made a point of keeping within earshot of his bell. I suppose they found it comforting.

The term 'belling the cat' refers to a similar dual function of a bell, in this instance the little round brass bell attached by a ribbon to the neck of a pet cat. The bell is a safeguard against the cat getting lost (as though a cat ever would if it didn't want to!) but it would also seem to ensure that the cat will never catch a mouse. How the cat must hate it!

Pop-gun Percy

May 1986

Though he naturally experiences some difficulty in relating to our way of life that is so different from his own one-hundred-and-twenty years ago, my great-grandfather William is always interested to hear of current events when we meet for a chat down the orchard, under the old apple-tree where his cider-press used to stand. Our last encounter occurred a few days after the American raid on Libya, so of course he wanted to hear about that.

Having elicited from me the salient details, he cogitated awhile and then embarked on the expected pronouncement. 'It reminds me a bit ....' he began, and I resigned myself to reminiscences of the American Civil War or the Franco-Prussian War, about both of which I had heard on previous occasions.

But no....'It reminds me a bit of old Pop-Gun Percy....!' Here was a character I had not previously met, and as he sounded decidedly interesting I gave great-grandfather his head, without interruption.

'It was Samuel Mudgkin, of course, who was the cause of the trouble–same as he was of most of the things that went wrong in Nadderbourne in those days. It was he who burned down Parsonage Farm when, coming home drunk, he climbed up into the hayloft and dropped off to sleep, thinking he'd got home. He was carrying an old horn lantern with a candle in it, and when the candle burned low it set fire to the hay. The old duffer was lucky to get out alive.

Some people remembered, too, when as a hobbledehoy he went to work at Nadderbourne Hall, doing odd jobs in the kitchen. It wasn't long before he had, somehow or another, acquired a key to the wine cellars and was making good use of it. His luck didn't last long. As he was blithely tripping down the stone steps to the cellars one quiet afternoon he met Sir Percival Wigg-Biddlecombe coming up.

'Hey, you boy, where d'y think you're going?' demanded the baronet.
'Back up, sir,' said Samuel.

There ended his job at Nadderbourne Hall. He never kept any job very long, but he got by comfortably enough with casual work, engaging in bits of dubious trading and, above all, poaching. There wasn't a trick he didn't know about the ways of helping himself to Sir Percival's pheasants, hares, partridges, and deer, and he was at it all the time. No close season for game in Samuel's book.

The keepers were constantly on the watch for him, but he hardly ever got caught. As far as I remember, he went to gaol only once, and then only for a month, after being convicted on circumstantial evidence. It was a kind of war between Sir Percival and his keepers on the one hand and Samuel on the other, with Samuel scoring most of the points and Sir Percival growing more and more exasperated.

Samuel had a ready market for his 'acquisitions'. A town poulterer took whatever he could deliver and passed on supplies not only to the local hotels but to customers in London. One day after lunching at his London club Sir Percival complimented the manager (an old friend) on the roast pheasant. 'I wouldn't wonder if it came from your part of the country,' smiled the manager. And, enquiring about the matter when he got home, Sir Percival found it was probably true.

'I've had just about enough of Samuel Mudgkin!' he shouted, and, seizing a double-barrelled shotgun he rushed down to the village, strode into Samuel's yard and blazed away with both barrels at Samuel's hens. Killed about a dozen of them.

Of course, within an hour everybody in the village knew about it, and after the next market day the tale was all over the county. The first reaction was stunned disbelief. Gradually, though, the realization sank in that Sir Percival had somehow lost status. He had put himself on the same level as Samuel Mudgkin. From being Sir Percival, lord of the manor, he had become Old Pop-Gun Percy. That is what everyone, from his fellow gentry to Samuel's grandchildren, called him till his dying day. Behind his back, of course.

What happened? Oh, nothing much. A little while afterwards he resigned as a JP. I suppose it was put to him that he couldn't very well judge poachers when he did the same thing himself.

Samuel came out of it not too badly. He said nothing, and didn't need to. Within a week there were just as many hens as before scratching about in his yard. He was related to half the village, see. Everyone knew what an old rascal he was, but he was one of themselves, so naturally they helped him out. And he carried on poaching, as though nothing had happened. Right into his old age.

Pop-Gun Percy once mentioned the incident to me, a long time afterwards, when he was getting old, too. I had just been paying the rent, me being one of his tenants, you see.

'That old business of Samuel Mudgkin and the hens,' he reflected, a bit defensively. 'I've been thinking a lot about it recently, and I'm sure I was right in what I did. I had to do it. It was logical, you know, now wasn't it?'

'Yes, sir,' I agreed. 'What you did was logical.'

Pop-Gun Percy seemed satisfied. Then he added, 'I wish, though, I'd never done it. Many times I've wished that. I lost, really, didn't I?' he said sadly.

'Yes, sir,' I agreed. 'You lost.'

Let the birds come to you

September 1984

W H Hudson once remarked that he had walked all day in an extensive wood in Wiltshire without seeing anything at all unusual, except a hare. And in my experience a hare in the middle of a wood is not all that unusual: I have quite often seen one in woodland rides, presumably taking a short cut from one block of arable land to another.

Like Hudson, however, I have frequently been struck by the paucity of bird life in large woods. On most days I walk in a forest near my home, often at this time of the year without seeing more than flights of woodpigeons overhead, a blackbird or two and perhaps an irate jay. I qualify the statement by 'at this time of year' because in May I expect to see or hear woodcock, nightjars, nightingales, willow warblers and various other woodland birds. Most of them are probably still there in late summer but undetectable because they are skulking silently in the deep recesses of the wood, away from rides and paths.

In fact, I know that they are, because the other day I saw a lot of them. Sauntering along a ride where I had walked a dozen times recently without seeing anything I suddenly became aware of numbers of small birds flitting about in the trees just ahead. I crept forward till I was in the midst of the group, stood with my back to a tree-trunk and waited.

Within the next ten minutes I identified seventeen species of woodland birds (the actual list comprised five species of tit, chaffinch, willow warbler, nuthatch, hedge sparrow, robin, great spotted woodpecker, blackbird, goldcrest, bullfinch, wren, tree-creeper and blackcap) and estimate that there were at least a hundred individuals in the gipsy caravan.

Each of them was industriously foraging, some on the floor of the forest, some high in the leaf canopy, some on the tree-trunks, some in the undergrowth. Every one was in constant motion, not staying to give a thorough examination to anything but simply snapping up any insect its sharp eyes happened to spot, but obviously finding plenty to eat. Then all had passed on, and the forest around me reverted to its normal state of vacuity.

I resumed my walk, delighted with the visitation and pleased with yet another vindication of one of the rules of bird-watching that I formulated many years ago. It is that to see the birds resident in a wood (outside of the nesting season) all one has to do is to remain stationary at one spot. In due course they will all come foraging around you. How quickly they arrive depends on the size of the wood.

The incident set me reviewing my other rules for bird-watching, devised from experience, and I pass them on as having, I think, a universal application:

1. This is an amplification of the one mentioned above. Learn to stand still. Birds react instinctively to sudden movement, but small birds in particular will pay little attention to a human who has learned how to 'freeze'. I have had tits actually perching on my shoulder, regarding me as an acceptable part of the scenery, like a fence post.

2. Go alone, or with one companion at the most. Communal rambles by field clubs and natural history societies may be popular social events, but the dedicated bird-watcher will do better to remember a previous engagement. Remember that a bird's eyes are six or eight times more efficient than yours and that to them you appear enormous. One such monster invading a bird's domain is alarming enough, but a whole horde of them, chattering at nineteen to the dozen, is calculated to send a bird diving for cover or fleeing to the uttermost parts of the wood.

3. Go early in the morning. Birds and indeed nearly all wild life have learned that humans in general are late risers. On the other hand, wild creatures wake at daybreak, eager for a meal. Experience has taught them that, as a rule, they can have the world to themselves for a few hours before we lay-abeds start to stir. The early bird catches the worm, and the early bird-watcher is there to see it happen.

4. Have access to the right places. There is nothing more disconcerting than to be interrupted, just as you are training your field-glasses on an apparent rarity, by an authoritative voice demanding what you are doing here. The man may be quite sympathetic and cooperative when you have explained to him, but by that time the bird has disappeared. Remember that most land in most parts of the world is somebody's property. If you feel like fighting a battle for the freedom of the countryside, you are entitled to do so, but don't try to mix it with bird-watching. If you intend to venture on private property, get permission first.

5. Learn how to identify birds by their plumage. It is as well to remember that the bird is likely to see you before you see it, and so your most probable view of it is a rear one as it flies away. Learn to distinguish

the pattern of white feathers displayed by each species. Two or three white feathers in wing or tail, as in the chaffinch or meadow pipit among English birds, are of more value in identification than large patches of red or purple. And the white rump sported by so many species is a real bonus.

6. Learn how to identify birds by their silhouettes and flight patterns. Not much practice is required to distinguish the dipping flight of woodpeckers or the slow flapping of herons, but after a time you will appreciate that every bird has its distinctive features detectable in flight and you will be able to recognise them with a fair degree of certainty, even when they are not much more than specks in the sky.

7. Learn to identify birds by their calls. I refer not only to their songs, which are used for only a few months each year, but to their call-notes. Once when I was preparing to give a talk on birds to a blind audience I particularly noted, on my morning walk, how many species I could identify by their calls only. The total was nineteen out of twenty-six. And now that my hearing is deteriorating I feel the deprivation.

My three final rules concern bird-watchers who, like myself, patrol the same path most days. You soon get to know what to expect and to realise when one species is missing. So:

8. Anticipate what you may see and look especially for it if you don't.

9. Never neglect the commonplace. Keep your eyes open for the commonest birds, and sooner or later you will see any rarities there may be about. Besides, there is still a lot to be learnt about the common ones.

10. Don't cheat. If you keep a check-list there is a temptation to tick off some of the common species, on the grounds that you will be sure to see them before the walk is over. But perhaps you won't. And then you will wonder what has happened to them and try to find explanations for their absence, and before you realise it you have discovered something new about these commonplace birds of the countryside.

Sleeping well on a stormy night

June 1985

Apprehensive of imminent cuts in production, as surpluses pile up into the popularly termed 'grain mountain', Britain's arable farmers are urgently casting around for alternative crops to the traditional wheat, barley and oats. They have already found one winner, oilseed rape, and at this year's Royal Show at Stoneleigh they will be able to study demonstrations of six others. These are lupins, linseed, soya beans, sun flowers, fenugreek and evening primrose.

Lupins have already gained some acceptance and could have a prosperous future. Linseed I grew for a time during the war and rapidly lost any enthusiasm I had for it. Varieties of soya beans and sunflowers that really suit the British climate have yet to be evolved. And with evening primrose and fenugreek the potential market, mostly in the pharmaceutical industry, is so far highly speculative.

But one crop which is apparently much neglected, in that the end users of it tell me they cannot get enough of it, is straw for thatch. It should be all the more attractive in that it is virtually a by-product; you can have your bundles of thatching straw and a good crop of wheat as well.

One reason for the lack of interest is the traditional association of thatch with so much that is obsolete. In the rural heritage for which I was reared thatch was the standard protection against wet weather. Farm workers, and I with them, used to spend days on end pulling out and tying up bundles of thatch ('yealms' in our local parlance). We used them for thatching hay-ricks, corn-ricks, mangold-heaps, cottages, barns, farmhouses, garden walls, and anything else that needed a hat. It was a poor man's necessity.

'I am a poor man; sythe I can not tyle my house I must be fayne to thatche it', wrote a person named Palsgrave, some four hundred years ago. He could never have foreseen, any more than I could, fifty years ago, the time when it would become a rich man's luxury. Back in 1880 when the villagers of Reydon, near Southwold, Suffolk, needed to repair their church roof by the most economical means possible, they tiled the side nearest the road but thatched the far side, where no-one would see it!

For the first seventeen years of my married life I lived in a little thatched farmhouse. When my American son-in-law came to see the place where his wife had been born he thought it was like a dolls' house. The outer walls are of chalk cob, two feet thick; the inner ones of wattle hurdle-work, covered with plaster. You can see the adze marks on the great, rough-hewn ceiling beams. The beams, the timbers in the walls and the floors are all of old oak. Thatch and hurdles, cob and oak, the place seems to have grown up naturally from its native soil.

It was pleasant to live in, too, for thatch is an excellent insulating material – warm in winter, cool in summer. We had to share it, though, with the wild life of the countryside. Birds nested in the thatched eaves and roosted there on winter nights. Insects from their abandoned nests crept in by way of the windows. There were bats roosting in the roof, woodlice invaded the house from the ivy on the walls, and snails strolled in under the door. But that's what you expect when you live in the country.

I asked my thatcher friend what it would cost nowadays to give the old house a new coat of thatch. He estimated between £4,200 and £5,000.

'The standard price runs at about £300 per 100 square feet,' he said, 'and for a cottage roof you can take an average of 1,400 square feet.'

The straw thatch bundles which I used to pull and bind for a few pence now cost £2 each. Thatching spars cost £40 a thousand. A sound coat of thatch should last for thirty years, though usually the roof is renewed piecemeal.

No wonder so many old thatched farm buildings have been demolished. When I was living in my little farmhouse it occupied one side of a quadrangle, the other sides being formed by barns, stable, implement sheds and woodsheds, all thatched. All were pulled down some twenty-five years ago, for the reason that to renew their thatch would have even then been uneconomic, though if they had managed to survive just a few more years they might have had a new lease of life as desirable country residences.

As a commercial crop on the farm, thatch has to possess certain qualities. Most of the new, short-strawed, high-yielding varieties of wheat will not do. The best variety is the old-fashioned Squareheads Master, which we used to grow on our farm when I was a boy.

'Good, strong, clean straw, five feet long,' enthused my thatcher friend. 'You can't beat it.'

Naturally it doesn't give grain yields equal to those of modern varieties, but, on the other hand, the thatch at £2 a bundle and a hundred bundles per acre should be an adequate compensation for loss of yield.

Of course, you cannot harvest the crop with a combine-harvester. The wheat has to be cut by a binder, and the sheaves ought to be left in stooks in the field for three weeks to dry. Then, later in the winter, the ricks are dismantled and the sheaves fed one by one into a threshing-machine equipped with a reed-comber, which beats the grain out of the ears but leaves the straw intact.

Thatch so prepared bears the technical name of reed-thatch. If you want a roof of real reed, of the sort that grows in lakes, you ask for Norfolk reed, though it doesn't necessarily grow in Norfolk. Thatching with Norfolk reed is more expensive, for the reason that the thatcher has to strip off any old thatch and get down to the basic battens. But it lasts much longer - say, a hundred years.

Thatching today offers a good living to an expert practitioner, and numbers of young men have taken it up. Calling for manual skill, expertise and devotion, it tends to be a vocation rather than a job. There is an old story of thatchers who, applying for an attractive contract, were asked to state their qualifications. The winner simply said, 'I can sleep well on a stormy night!'

Perhaps it is legitimate to speculate as to whether modern generations whose surname is derived from the ancient craft inherit in some way the same proud qualities!

I feel I have to add, though, the comment made by one cynical listener to whom I recounted the story. 'Perhaps,' he said, 'the rascal knew he had made such a botched job of it that now he was sure of a winter's work, repairing the damage! '

On the up and up

December 1983

The archaeologists, antiquarians, folklorists and other authorities who puzzle over the Nazca lines of Peru and similar phenomena are, it seems to me, being uncharacteristically obtuse. What is the point, we ask them, of laboriously constructing intricate patterns on the landscape that can only be appreciated from the air?

We have some examples in England, notably the Berkshire White Horse, which looks more like a surrealistic alley-cat slinking up over the brow of the hill than like a horse, and if it exists, the Glastonbury Zodiac. It makes no sense, reply the experts, because our remote ancestors who made these monuments could not fly. Ah, but couldn't they?

My son in British Columbia regularly risks life and limb, to the abiding disapproval of his wife and mother, by taking to the air in one of those powered hang-gliders called 'microlites'. Before he acquired this machine he experimented with an unpowered hang-glider. Equipped with these spectacular wings, you jump hopefully off the edge of a cliff and rely on an ascending air current to deposit you gently on the solid earth.

I doubt whether it would have been beyond the skill and ingenuity of our remote ancestors to devise a hang-glider. They possessed the necessary materials, which are cloth, rope and supple rods, at the time of the building of Stonehenge, and, as Dr Alexander Thom has demonstrated during the past few decades, they were highly gifted mathematicians who knew about Pythagorian triangles at least a thousand years before Pythagoras. The ancient legends of Icarus and other alleged astronauts may have a basis in fact, after all.

And so, may the tale of Eadmer, a monk of Malmesbury, related by William of Malmesbury in the twelfth century, who attached wings to his arms and jumped off the abbey tower in a vain attempt to fly, for he fell and broke both his legs and was lame ever afterwards. He put his failure down to the fact that he forgot to provide himself with a tail– and he may have been right, at that.

It is not impossible that he was following instructions preserved in an ancient manuscript in the Abbey. I seem to remember, too, that when Marco Polo was travelling in Tibet, in the thirteenth century, he was entranced by the monks who, attached to what he calls kites, launched themselves from the terrifying Himalayan precipices and successfully flew.

These thoughts went through my mind when floating aloft in a glider with one of my sons-in-law, who is an experienced glider-pilot. Once the tug and pull of the launching-rope (assuming the machine is launched by a tractor, as ours was), is over, a glider gives one a buoyant sense of freedom and weightlessness. And one becomes aware, too, of new elements in the environment – the existence of invisible air currents which are key factors in one's chances of survival.

I have, of course, often marked the evidence for the existence of these currents from the ground. Thermals are easy to observe. Only the other morning I saw a party of wheeling gulls taking advantage of a thermal over our village, a thermal created by ascending air currents from chimneys and central heating apparatus. On moderately tranquil days the thermal moves gradually downwind from the source, and the birds follow.

It was enthralling to be up there in the glider, sharing the skies with the birds, though only once or twice did I see a gull sailing alongside us for a few moments. When we came down to land, however, we encountered much more impressive and indeed alarming evidence of things invisible. I nearly wrote 'concrete evidence', for above the airfield tarmac (this was in late summer) we seemed to hit something like a concrete wall.

The glider bucked and swayed and I think would have plummetted to the ground but for the skill of the pilot. In his able hands the machine recovered its equilibrium, and we soared around for a further twenty minutes before approaching the landing-ground from another angle and coming down on grass instead of asphalt.

'I might have known,' said the pilot apologetically. 'Thermals rise from any warm surface, even from a ploughed field heated by the sun, and from tarmac they can be pretty deadly.'

If only air were visible, what fantastic patterns we would see in the sky! Great undulating waves as the air attempts to level out after crossing a mountain barrier; glider pilots say that the waves created by the Welsh mountains are discernible as far east as Bedfordshire. Spiralling thermals over every building, merging into big ones over towns. Tiny thermals over such insignificant features as human beings. You have only to walk in the woods in summer to appreciate that shoals of flies quickly discover a thermal above your head.

Every man produces his own thermal. It can be measured by a

sufficiently sensitive thermometer. Which is why I am saddened whenever in winter I wait for a train on a draughty station platform. Around me I see men who ought to know better – not young, vigorous men with a good head of hair, but elderly citizens with wispy grey hair hardly sufficient to cover their bald pates – standing around without hats.

What a stupid fashion this hatless craze is. Our body heat rises, as all heat does, and, given the chance, will escape in a private little thermal from the top of our head. One would think that we would at least have the sense to put a lid on it.

In praise of bulls

September 1984

Never, I suppose, in the history of the world has there been a more compassionate age than ours. Our enlightened concern extends far beyond our own species to embrace virtually every other creature with which we share our planet.

Consciences are exercised over the poultry and pigs in factory farms, over seals bludgeoned to death on Canadian ice, over deer and foxes pulled down in the chase, over assorted animals employed in laboratory experiments, over creatures in cages and creatures in traps and birds blown out of the boundless sky to collapse earthwards in bloody bundles of feathers. Our compassion goes as far as liberating caged mink (than which there are no more bloodthirsty animals in all creation), and the most recent object of our pity is the dolphin, which we are now told is inconsolably unhappy in a dolphinarium.

But one animal excluded from all this goodwill is the bull. At least, the bulls we can see for ourselves. We can work up some compassion for the bulls who meet their end in Spanish and Latin American bull-rings, but they are many miles away, not confined to a bull-pen on the nearest farm or patrolling a meadow just down the road. The latter, we feel, would be much better removed from that meadow and shut up in the bull-pen, preferably behind rails of tubular steel.

I have a soft spot for bulls, probably because they featured quite prominently in my early life. The village bull, available for service by all the herds in the parish, lived on my father's farm, and when I left school in my teens I became his custodian. I tended and learned to respect, even like, a succession of bulls, regretting my job only when neighbours insisted on bringing their cows for service on Sunday mornings or Christmas Day.

The dairyman who was my predecessor was frightened by bulls, and, no matter how he tried to conceal it, the bulls knew and played him up accordingly. They never tried the games with me, simply, I suppose, because it had never occurred to me to be afraid of them.

I remember that once I was completely at the mercy of one of our bulls. As I unfastened his chain to release him from his stall and let him out for his daily exercise I stepped back on to a slab of broken concrete and keeled over with a sprained ankle. There I lay, curled up with pain on the floor, and there stood the bull, loose and looking down at me. Summoning my most authoritative voice, I told him firmly to get out .... and he did.

On another occasion a bull did get loose and escape into the village street, on a market day just as the road was crowded with people on their way to the bus stop. Hearing the commotion my wife hurried from the kitchen and arrived on the highway to see pedestrians scattering in all directions while the bewildered bull came trotting towards her. Seizing a flimsy stick, she stood in the middle of the road and commanded the animal to stop .... which he did. Then she quietly guided him into a nearby meadow.

Bulls are like children or dogs. They belong to us, and they look to us for guidance. Being mischief-loving males, they will test us, to see what they can get away with, but, confronted with authority, they will obey. There are, of course, rogue bulls. A farmer who has had considerable experience with bulls, rearing them in some numbers for bull beef, has put the incidence of trouble-making bulls at one in eighty. Probably no higher than the ratio of human trouble-makers.

Some breeds tend to be more temperamental than others, the dairy breeds more so than the beef breeds. At an agricultural show we may see a massive, white-faced Hereford bull led into the ring by a rope, at the other end of which is a slip of a girl. But the Jersey bull which follows, though much smaller, needs two strong men with poles to control him.

I sometimes smile at the subterfuge of a farming friend who, when one of his pastures starts to produce a crop of mushrooms, turns an old Hereford bull loose in it. I help myself to the mushrooms, for the docile old chap is as quiet as a sheep - a good deal less aggressive than some rams I have known. But I wouldn't venture if the bull were a Freisian, unless it was a bull I happened to know and who knew me.

The luckiest bulls in Britain are those young beef bulls, mostly Hereford, who run with herds of heifers to help them produce their first calves. Contented with the natural life they are leading, they may walk over to inspect an intruder but are unlikely to display any aggression, though they may object to dogs.

The areas of Britain where they can roam free, however, are becoming more and more restricted, as ramblers, having neglected to fasten a gate or two, complain about such dangerous animals being left at large. The place for bulls, as far as the public is concerned, is in concrete behind brick walls and steel rails, though to us, if we were at the receiving end, such a place would be called a gaol. Or, if we were thinking about a hen, it would be a battery cage.

Nor are the bulls at cattle breeding stations, otherwise artificial insemination centres, any more fortunate. An outstanding bull selected for such an honour may become the sire of thousands of calves, but he himself derives little satisfaction from the process. For him life is an endless series of masturbations. From his night quarters in a cell he is

taken by day to a pasture and there tethered with a score of other bulls, whom he would naturally regard as his rivals. He can see them all but cannot get at them for the trial of strength which his instinct tells him ought to be staged. What frustration!

Fundamentally the bull is the patriarch of a family. The best example in Britain of a bull in its natural state is provided by the wild cattle of Chillingham (Northumberland). Of them Professor H C Pawson writes:

> The cattle feed mainly in the evening and when they move, do so in file, the 'king' leading, cows and calves forming the centre, and other bulls to the rear .... The calf is dropped in a secluded spot and remains hidden, being suckled two or three times daily, until it is brought into the herd by the dam at about a week to a fortnight old, being first met by the 'king', who escorts them in person, when the mother and new arrival are duly inspected and approved by the other ladies of the herd .... If thoroughly alarmed, the herd stampedes in a well-arranged formation of cows in front, calves next, then the bulls, with the 'king' bull in the rear of all.

That is the bull at home. Not an over-aggressive animal. Gentle with his cows, tolerant with their calves, but ready at any time to do battle for them.

Men have treated bulls far worse than bulls have treated men. They have taken away from innumerable bulls their masculinity, by castration. They have baited them cruelly, for sport. They still kill thousands annually in the ritual spectacle of the bull-ring. Simply because they can think of no other way of controlling them they confine these splendid animals to steel-barred cells or restrict their movement by short tethers.

There is no indignity they have not heaped upon them, and yet they fear their victims. The bull is one of the few animals, ruthlessly exploited by man, who, given the chance, has the power to retaliate.

If man possessed that massive, muscular power he knows how he would be tempted to use it, and he supposes that the bull would do the same. But the bull is not like that. He is a gentler creature altogether.

The fate of fetes

July 1983

One hopes, though without much conviction, that other village fetes are better organised than a summer event in a village in which I have a special interest.

The hard-pressed secretary, called away to deal with the latest crisis, was constrained to leave the tombola stall in the charge of his son Kevin and two other boys, James and Jonathan, all aged about eight or nine. As they had been helping him they knew the ropes and managed very well. After a time Kevin, inspecting the till, announced, 'Well, we've done very well so far, I think you can now go off for a time, Jonathan. Come back in half-an-hour.'

With that he scooped a couple of handfuls of cash out of the till and transferred them to Jonathan, who quickly vanished into the crowd. The tombola stall continued to do good business. Being a loyal and reliable lad, Jonathan turned up at the end of the stipulated half-hour, with sundry trophies but, naturally, no cash left.

'Now it's your turn, James,' said the efficient Kevin, and James was despatched into the melee well fortified with cash. Lastly, James and Jonathan held the fort while Kevin went on a spending spree.

Towards the end of the afternoon Kevin's father returned and was immediately immersed in running the stall. Neither he nor anyone else noticed that the takings, or what was left of them, were less than might have been expected. No-one would ever have known if at bedtime Kevin, in all innocence, had not related to his mother what had happened. She was both amused and startled.

'How can you explain to boys of that age that what they did was wrong?' she asked her husband. 'I tried to, but Kevin objected that they did spend all the money at the fete, and wasn't that what was wanted?' So in the end they put a pound or two of their own money into the cash box and closed the incident.

Once when visiting a youth club in the Ivory Coast I was impressed by the amount of money they told me they had raised by cultivating a 'God's Acre'.

'And what are you going to do with the money?' I asked.

'Oh, we've already spent it. We've ordered the second biggest bell in West Africa for our church!'

I thought, what a warped idea of priorities, in a country where there is so much human need! But, as I have often noticed, when I make a critical judgement of that sort, I get presented with a situation which makes me eat my words. Hardly had I settled down again in an English village before I was invited to take part in the local summer fete.

'Of course. By the way, what is it in aid of?'

'Oh, we're going to rehang the church bells!'

I did register a mild protest, recounting my West African experience.

'Well, yes, I can appreciate that point of view,' the rector admitted. 'But surely the main thing here is to get the people working together as a community? '

By that criterion, which is probably as valid as any, Kevin and his mates can stand vindicated. And lucky boys they are indeed, to live in a village community which involves itself in organising a fete (or 'summer fayre' as it is more often called nowadays). As I myself did, when I was a boy.

Village fetes, by whatever name, have a very respectable lineage. John Aubrey, the antiquary, writing in the time of Charles I, before the Commonwealth had interfered with so many of the old customs, comments:

> In every parish is (or was) a church house, to which belonged spits, crocks, etc., utensils for dressing provisions. Here the housekeepers met and were merry, and gave their charity. The young people were there, too, and had dancing, bowling, shooting at the butts, etc., the ancients sitting gravely by and looking on ....

The events were called Church Ales in those days, but, apart from the archery, the programme seems to have been much the same as for twentieth century village fetes. Anyone who has participated in one of the latter would have felt quite at home at a Church Ale when Shakespeare's genius was still in full spate and before the first King Charles was decapitated.

Nowadays we pay lip service to democracy. At a village meeting some time during the winter a committee, with chairman, vice-chairman, treasurer and secretary, is elected. The number of parishioners keen enough to turn out on a winter evening being limited, the committee usually comprises all those present. Sub-committees, with specific responsibilities, are then hived off – there is a sub-committee for organising the fancy dress procession, another for the sports, another for laying out the ground and setting up the stalls, another for the teas. For everything the proper procedure is observed, or, as John Aubrey puts it, 'all things were civil and without scandal.'

Although no-one would dream of suggesting such a thing, precisely the same results could be achieved by someone (the chairman or secretary) visiting certain key characters and remarking, 'I take it you'll be doing the same as last year!'

Woe betide anyone who proposes prising Mrs Wandle away from the tea tent, which she has organised for the past thirty years, and her mother before her. Or usurping the position of Bob Puttock, who considers himself a dab hand at running the sports and whose eighteen stone make him the ideal anchorman for the tug-of-war against that upstart lot in the neighbouring parish.

And who wants a television personality to come and open the fete when Lady Stourchester, up at the big house, is ready and willing, as she has been ever since her marriage some forty years ago?

Preparations reach their crescendo on the Friday evening before the fete, always a Saturday event, when all save a few curmudgeonly misanthropes swarm like bees in and around the village hall and the meadow.

On Saturday noon the weather, which has held fine for the past fortnight, suddenly collapses in a paroxysm of tears. Lady Stourchester makes her opening speech to the accompaniment of a diapason of rain rattling on the corrugated iron roof of the village hall; the tea tent is permanently overcrowded by refugees from the downpour; the tug-of-war stalwarts flex their muscles by manhandling cars in and out of the muddy meadow that serves as a car park.

Disaster? No. At the next meeting of the committee, the week after the fete, the treasurer rises to announce a modest profit. The meeting congratulates itself on achieving such a result in defiance of the weather and launches straight away into fixing the date of and discussing ideas for next year's fete.

Of such stuff is the English character fashioned, and has been for centuries. Kevin, James and Jonathan are lucky little lads.

A 'success' story

December 1987

It must have been ten or twelve years ago that I first met Barry and Val Cornward. My old friend Stan Drewett introduced them to me. Stan farms over at Wellhouse, and these people Cornward had bought a little place of thirty acres or so next to him. They had come to him for advice, and few farmers (or anyone else, for that matter) can resist that approach.

They were a likeable couple. The reason for their descent into the countryside showed in Barry's face. Following a heart attack, a doctor had given him a dire warning: ease off or take the consequences. Barry had been a successful businessman in something or other in London, but the years of stress had taken their toll.

The idea of a complete break with urban and suburban life had appealed to him and Val. Reaction from the scare was an element in Barry's decision, but for Val there were no reservations. Plump and competent, she looked a typical countrywoman, as probably her ancestors had been a few generations back. As for the children, Jason and Kate, they revelled in the prospect. Ponies!

Under Stan's tutelage, they settled in. Their investments were all-embracing. They bought five Jersey cows, two in-pig sows, fifty pullets on point-of-lay, half-a-dozen black Jacob sheep, some geese and a guinea-fowl, a few hutches of rabbits and, of course, the ponies. Stan pointed out that they were setting out to spend their lives as caterers to a bunch of farm animals, but that was what they wanted. In cord trousers, rubber boots, and an anorak Barry humped about trusses of hay and buckets of swill, while Val helped with the milking and learned to skim off the cream and to make yoghurt.

As the days lengthened the work multiplied. On the two or three little arable fields there were crops to be sown, after due cultivations. The Cornwards' concept of country living insisted that in the kitchen garden every conceivable vegetable and herb, from artichokes to zucchinis, must be grown. The milk resulting from the lush grass of the May meadows was so rich that Val felt she must make butter, and that in addition to rearing broods of chicken and other assorted livestock. The little farm was alive with the clucking of hens, the honking of the protective but harassed gander, the crowing of cocks, the bleating of lambs, the squealing of impatient pigs and the chatter of two happy children who were delighted with it all.

Before the Cornwards were ready for it the grass was ready to cut for hay, and then, with hardly a break, it was time for harvest. Stan, watching the pageant unfold with a tolerant eye, sent his men and machinery down to give a hand when he judged it necessary, but before summer was really established Val found herself having to get up at four o'clock in the morning to fit in the butter-making. Not that she minded; the countryside was lovely in the early morning.

However, summer also brought visitors – friends and relations from their former life. That is one of the hazards of country living, as migrants from the city soon discover. To satisfy the natural desire of the visitors to go home laden with country goodies, Val became proficient at plucking and dressing poultry. The chores piled up to the extent that she obviously needed help, and so, at Stan's instigation, Edith arrived on the scene.

Edith, a somewhat lumpy country lass, was well versed in country lore and proved invaluable. She and Val worked happily in harness together, steered competently through the exacting Christmas period and pushed cheerfully into the Cornwards' second year. The rising sap of spring brought an accustomed crop of spots and pimples on Edith's adolescent complexion, and Val remarked on them. Then, one day, she noticed that they had vanished.

'How?' she asked.

'Oh, some stuff my Gran makes,' Edith told her. Goose grease was apparently a major ingredient.

Val experimented and found that the remedy was indeed effective. It was an interesting challenge. She improved 'Gran's' recipes with essential fragrant oils from her herb garden, and scoured the town shops for attractive pots and jars to hold the mixture. When the summer visitors come, she thought, I shall have something new and exciting to offer them.

The visitors agreed. The demand grew until Barry sat up and took notice of his wife's new hobby. 'Hey! we've got a gold-mine here!' he exclaimed.

His dormant business instincts and experience were resurrected. Feeding pigs and milking cows soon began to seem a waste of valuable time. He was busy concocting schemes for launching his range of cosmetic products on the market. If I were to mention their name you would probably recognise them instantly.

The farm was too small. Edith and her boyfriend, to whom she wished to get married, were installed there to run a specialised unit for

producing herbs and geese. Somewhat reluctantly Val agreed to move to a larger house, away from the clutter of the kitchen-cum-factory. New premises were acquired to manufacture and package the stuff on the scale required. When last I saw Barry it was in his plush new office in London, while Val was back in a suburban home (though a far more up-market one than formerly) so that Barry should not have too long a daily commuting journey.

I invited five friends to read this story and asked for their comments. Four thought it a 'good, conventional success story'.

One, an elderly person, found it 'inexpressibly sad'.

So do I.

Birthday at Lammas-tide

August 1986

'The largest artificial mound in Europe' is the definition given by *The Guinness Book of Records* to Silbury Hill, the site of which occupies five and a half acres in my home county, Wiltshire. Lying just over a mile south of the gigantic stone circle of Avebury, Silbury is an earthen cone or pyramid, 130 feet high, the making of which involved moving 670,000 tons of chalk, a task which required an estimated 18 million hours of work by men using antler picks. Presented with these formidable facts, our obvious reaction is to ask,–why?

Many attempts have been made to find the answer. On the grounds that it resembles a giant round-barrow, a popular theory has been that it is a burial mound. Local lore claims that it was raised over the grave of a King Sil, who was buried there, sitting on his horse and surrounded by vast treasure. So from 1776 onwards a series of excavators have probed Silbury, sinking shafts from top to bottom and driving tunnels into the very centre of the hill.

The most comprehensive investigation of all was conducted by Professor Richard Atkinson and the BBC in 1968 and 1969. Months of patient work, in full view of television cameras, failed to reveal King Sil in his golden armour or any other burial. Summarising the dig, Professor Atkinson wrote, 'No trace of any structure, deposit or ancient disturbance was found in the small area near the centre which had not previously been disturbed.'

Evidently Silbury was not a burial mound, but the question remained 'What, then, was it?'

Recently I have been browsing through a book, published in 1976 but which I have previously missed seeing, entitled *The Silbury Treasure*, by author Michael Danes, who is convinced he knows the answer. The hill is, he says, the Mother Goddess herself, of primitive religion.

Our ancestors in those far-off days had no notions of false modesty. The earth, they knew, produced the crops which kept them alive; women produced the children which ensured the continuity of the tribe; so the existence of an Earth Mother or Goddess was a logical inference.

The essential function of a mother is to give birth, so it seemed sensible to them to depict the goddess as a heavily pregnant woman, about to give birth. And that, says Mr Dames, is exactly what Silbury is. It is a huge, three-dimensional goddess in a squatting posture, and he quotes numerous examples of similar representations of the Earth Goddess from different cultures.

Nothing is ever simple, of course, and he believes that the ground plan at Silbury, as well as the hill itself, also represents a woman on the point of giving birth. Her form is outlined by the water which surrounds the hill. But there is even more to it than that. If, at the appropriate time, you stand on the terrace which surrounds the top of the hill you can witness the birth of the child which the goddess is bearing!

The sequence of events is as follows. At 7.35 pm the sun sets. At 8 pm the moon rises. The moon is the 'baby'. After its birth at 8pm, you can see it in various positions with relation to its mother, such as lying on her knee, until at ten minutes past midnight it reaches its maximum altitude. That, according to Mr Dames, was the moment for cutting the umbilical cord and probably for the ceremonial cutting of the first stalks of corn, which he thinks were probably growing in a sacred patch on top of the hill. It was, in fact, the signal for the beginning of harvest.

And what was this all-important date? Why, Lammas-tide. Nowadays Lammas falls on August 8, but to fit in with the less precise calendar of primitive men a margin of a week or two on either side has to be allowed. The key factor is that the festival was observed when the full moon rose within half-an-hour or so of sunset. And that occurs approximately midway between Midsummer and the autumnal equinox.

As I read this conjectural account of the origin and significance of Silbury all that I know about Lammas seemed to fall into place. At times, when speaking at Harvest Homes and Harvest Festivals, I have deplored the abolition of old-style August Bank Holiday, which fell on the first weekend of August. Though in its latter days it was simply a convenient date for a holiday, it did serve to perpetuate the ancient festival of Lammas, the traditional date for the gathering of first-fruits and so the beginning of harvest.

In Christian centuries the wheat grains from the first harvest field were quickly ground into flour and made into bread, in the form of little loaves. These were brought to church and presented to the priest at the altar. The celebration was called 'Loaf-mass', hence Lammas.

Six weeks or so later, at the end of harvest, the last stalks of corn were carefully cut and fashioned into a Corn Dolly or Kern Baby. Though straw-weaving now is a popular craft with Women's Institutes and other village organisations, the Corn Dolly was once a potent goddess, capable of giving life to the seed for the next harvest. That is why, after the winter solstice, she was gently laid in a furrow and buried by good soil. And originally she was fashioned from the corn cut at Lammas, not at the harvest's end.

The story of Silbury begins so very long ago. According to the latest estimates it is dated at 2745 BC, give or take about 200 years either way. But a few Lammas customs still linger, while others were abandoned within living memory. Some are concerned with tithes and the payment of rents; others with sheep fairs; others with festivities on hill tops.

In Orkney 'Lammas brothers and sisters' were couples who attended Kirkwall Lammas Fair and for that period behaved as though they were married. Manx people used to hold a somewhat scandalous celebration on the top of Snaefell at Lammas-tide, until, it is said, a Methodist preacher put an effective stop to it by passing round a collection bag!

I have never stood on top of the Silbury Hill at the rising of the

Lammas-tide full moon, and now I suppose increasing years make it unlikely that I ever shall. As with seeing the Midsummer sunrise at Stonehenge, you need a clear sky. But I am assured that, when conditions are right, you can still witness the Earth Mother giving birth to the moon, as she did to the satisfaction of those neolithic people who shifted all those tons of chalk and soil in her honour, nearly five thousand years ago.

The winners

September 1987

The resident colony of sparrows in my garden is now conspicuously absent at breakfast-time. At every other season of the year they are waiting at first light for the alms on which they exist, or rather thrive. Only in late summer and autumn are they content to leave the pickings to the blackbirds, tits, and marauding parties of starlings. But I know where they are. Just two short hedgerows away are harvest-fields, acres of them, replete with both grain and insects. The menu is evidently even more attractive than our daily offering of household scraps.

Around mid-day the truants stagger home, their little crops so bursting with good food that they can view with equanimity the bare bird-table. Lined up on the shed roof, they preen and chirp cheerily in the afternoon sun, until it is time for the evening excursion to the harvest-fields for supper. It is the sparrows' summer holiday, and how they enjoy it!

The winners in Nature's stakes are the species that can most readily adapt themselves, and none is more successful than the sparrow. Early on it must have been appreciated that the future belonged to this somewhat dangerous but incredibly versatile two-legged animal and so decided to throw in its lot with us.

Did it consciously make the decision? Presumably individual sparrows did, and I for one am not a bit surprised. For, looking at the species which have done well in the world, I think I detect evidence of intelligence above the ordinary in them.

My sparrows sun themselves on the shed roofs on warm summer afternoons, but where are they when it rains? Under the eaves! A convenient ledge, which is really the top of a timber-panelled fence, tucks neatly in under the wide eaves of the shed and provides a convenient roof for any birds clever enough to take advantage of it. There the sparrows line up on a wet day, comfortably surveying the downpour.

Now, do you know any other birds intelligent enough to take shelter from the rain? I don't think I do - at least, not in England. On wet days I often see bedraggled finches, robins, blackbirds, and other garden birds, but not sparrows.

We can classify starlings, too, as among the winners. Unlike the demure and ubobtrusive sparrows, they are noisy, vulgar, ostentatious birds. Nobody loves them, but an incident I witnessed the other day inclines me to give them high marks for adaptability. Peanut holders

are supposed to be for tits, woodpeckers, and nuthatches, though they also present no problems to greenfinches, which enjoy peanut above all other delicacies. In my garden peanut holders are for sparrows, too: they have long since mastered the art of clinging to the wire. And in hard weather last winter our resident chaffinches at long last grasped the idea.

From my window the other morning I saw an unfamiliar bird clinging to the holder and tucking in greedily to the pea-nuts. Fawnish-brown in colour, it was of starling build, but I couldn't believe it was a young starling until I focused the field-glasses.

I had previously seen adult starlings who had mastered the art of extracting pea-nuts, but on this occasion there were no adult starlings in sight. So this young bird must have taken note of the behaviour of the tits and sparrows and decided they were worth emulating. Which to my mind puts it in the Mensa IQ for birds. No wonder starlings are abundant.

A different quality is I think, responsible for the phenomenal spread of the collared dove which first began nesting in England (in Norfolk) in 1955 to become among the commonest and most familiar birds in lowland Britain.

Relaxing in an armchair one afternoon in early September I became aware of doves purring and cooing just outside my window. Idly I watched them courting and mating on the top timber of a pergola. Then I remembered that I had watched an exactly similar performance on a sunny afternoon in February. September-February – and every other month. For humans, it is said, kissing is out of season only when the gorse isn't in bloom, and apparently the same is true of the collared dove. A species which continues to breed all the year round may expect a population explosion.

As I write, the sky outside my window is alive with swallows and martins. I have broken off for a few moments to try to estimate the numbers of house-martins sunning themselves on a south-facing tiled roof across the road. Difficult because they are in constant motion, but there must be at least three hundred. And they are just a fraction of those insect-hawking in the air. Yet in the spring both swallows and martins seemed to be arriving so late and in such small numbers that I feared a disastrous decline.

For explanation I look to the remarkable adaptability of swallows and martins in the nesting season. Not for them the strict demarcation of the role of the sexes. When there are young to be fed, both parents pitch in. And not only that, but as one brood is reared the parents get busy on the next, and when the youngsters are hatched the first brood helps to feed them. So do aunts and cousins and all the rest of the tribe. And very often there is a third brood.

Never be surprised by anything you observe in the family life of swallows and martins, a wise old naturalist once told me. No wonder they can merit a place among the winners in Nature's stakes.

A fortune underground

October 1987

The other day a man arrived to pick my brains about the ancient craft of truffling and persuaded me to take him to the woods where, theoretically, there ought to be some. Well, it was a pleasant enough way of spending a leisure hour or two on a quiet autumn afternoon, but, alas, we came home without truffles.

I live in a village which was the last stronghold of English truffle-hunters. In 1860 a dozen or so trufflers' families lived there. They even petitioned Parliament, asking that their dogs be exempted from the 12 shillings annual dog tax .... 'We being poor labouring men, living in a woody district of the county where a great many English truffles grow, which we cannot find without dogs, we do therefore keep and use a small pudle sort of dog wholly and solely for that and no other .... It has been carried on by our ancestors for generations without paying tax for the dogs...'

The last of the truffle-hunters, Alfred Collins, whom I knew quite well, died in the 1950s but had not been very active at the craft for some 20 years previously. His father, Eli Collins, was a celebrated character, who had access to the woods on all the local estates. The contemporary Earl of Radnor, having satisfied himself that the truffle-hounds were so single-minded in their search for the underground fungus that they would not even look up at a startled pheasant, had a velveteen uniform designed and made for Eli. To see the uncanny skill of the dogs at work was a treat with which the Earl loved to entertain his house-guests.

Truffles are subterranean fungi of the genus *Tuber*. We have eight species in England, the best, from the point of view of culinary excellence being *Tuber aestivum*. They usually range in size from hazel-nut to a large tea-cup. The record is said to be about two and a half pounds. Gilbert White, in his Journals, referred quite frequently to trufflers working at Selborne and other places in Hampshire. A truffler would dig regularly at a small beech grove near Andover where he could be reasonably sure of finding seven or eight pounds of truffles. These were divided between the truffler and the landowner, Gilbert White's brother Henry. The price was then around half-a-crown a pound - a useful harvest for a farm labourer whose weekly wage was probably not more than three half-crowns.

Truffles now cost around £160 a pound! And that is the reason for the present resurgence of interest in them. A few hours' digging in the counterpart of Henry White's beech grove would, on that basis, yield the lucky truffler £1,120. And there is no reason to suppose that truffles are any less abundant than they were two hundred years ago. The problem is to find them.

The Hampshire and Wiltshire truffle-hunters relied on dogs...'a small pudle sort of dog'. Bing, the dog my wife owned before she was

married, was said by locals to be the 'spittin' image of them there little truffle dogs', by then extinct. He was a shaggy white mongrel, with evidently some terrier blood, but I doubt whether the authentic truffle-hounds were pure bred.

It doesn't matter. Any intelligent little dog with a good nose could be trained. From puppyhood all their food was smeared with truffles, so that they associated the scent of truffles with food. But the training period could last up to two years, and smearing puppy's food with truffles at £160 a pound for all that time would be prohibitive! Some enthusiasts, apparently, doubtless encouraged by the possible eventual returns on their investment, are thinking of doing just that.

Others have been seeking to tap the expertise of Continental experts. Our local truffle-dogs were said to have come originally from Spain (another legacy of the wrecked Armada) or, more probably, from France a century or two later. In France and Italy today both dogs and pigs are employed to locate truffles, and I heard recently of a French pig being imported for the purpose .... though with no notable successes scored to date.

My visitor the other day wondered whether truffles could be found by dowsing. Getting busy with his rods under suitable beeches he obtained positive reactions in a few places. We dug, but found no truffles. A minor problem is that there is no fixed rule about the depth at which the fungi grow. Some are just below the surface, others down 20 inches.

Truffles are in season from Michaelmas to Lady Day, though Gilbert White reports large numbers being found as early as July. Traditionally, they are associated with beech trees, but they also occur under hazel, hawthorn, sycamore and, I think, oak. The fact that in 1860 no fewer than 10 or 12 men in a single village were engaged in truffling implies that, as White says, truffles were abundant. I see no reason why they should not still be so. Forward, the optimists!

Lucky thirteen in a clutch of eggs

January 1982

Thirteen is the proper clutch of eggs for a broody hen to incubate. That is not because thirteen is the natural number of eggs for a hen to lay before she goes broody. Any hen worth her grain will do better than that. But any knowledgeable countryman, or rather countrywoman, will agree that it is imperative for a hen to be set on an *uneven* number of eggs, and, as fifteen are too many for her to cover and eleven too few, it must be thirteen. From time immemorial, certainly back to the Roman era, it has been considered unlucky to set twelve or fourteen eggs under a hen. Goodness knows why.

In this epoch of battery cages and mass-produced broilers it is surprising how many country folk still remember the old lore. Some even continue to practise it. For me the first three months of the year are always associated with hatching chicken. On the farm where I was reared the alert for broody hens to be reported immediately went out soon after Christmas. By February my mother generally had a dozen or so hens sitting on eggs in a collection of old apple barrels, orange boxes, tea chests and similar containers domiciled in a derelict cottage behind the big barn. Every morning she let them out in relays for an eating, drinking and scratching session, but by the end of half-an-hour they were ready to return to their nests.

For me as a boy spring would have been deficient if it had lacked newly hatched chicken. To tend a broody hen for three weeks and then one morning to put one's hand into the oven-like heat beneath her wings and find there a soft handful of powder-puff chicks amid a scatter of broken egg-shells and to feel more eggs already fractured by little birds awaiting birth, that is one of the supreme joys of country life.

A treasured photograph is of one of my daughters at the age of five peering into a hen-coop at newly hatched chicken whose bright eyes are peeping back at her from the shelter of a warm, feathered breast. That was a cosy heart-warming little experience which used to be the heritage of every country child. I wish it still were.

A population engaged in reproducing itself on the scale and at the pace of the human species at present needs the mass production of food to match, say the pundits, and I suppose they are right. Certainly poultry, from being something of a luxury on the table fifty years ago, has become one of the cheapest of meats. But I confess that some of the things that happen to poultry nowadays appal me.

The technique of sex linkage allows breeders to be ultra-efficent, to the extent of being able, by observing the colour of the down, to differentiate between cockerels and pullets at birth. So unwanted cockerels of an egg-laying strain can go straight from the incubator into the gas-bucket. By the thousand. As an old-fashioned sentimentalist, I confess that from dumping bright-eyed baby chicken into gas-buckets to consigning bright-eyed children to gas-chambers, as happened in Hitler's Germany, is for me an uncomfortably short step.

Chicken in an incubator are mere units. Chicken under a hen are individuals. We used to save them all, both pullets and cockerels, and took special care over any that were sickly or deformed. Being mongrels, they were all differently coloured and so could be recognised. We came to know them as individuals, and as such they developed personalities and characters, as a pet dog or cat will do. There were docile hens and vicious hens, placid ones and nervous ones, staid old matrons and flighty young flappers who were forever flirting around the cock.

Some of our hens developed surprising idiosyncracies. One slate-coloured hen acquired a taste for mice, which used to drop into an iron corn-bin for a feast of grain and were unable to get out. When anyone approached, Slatey would come scampering up, her head tilted alertly. We had only to turn the bin on its side, so that the mice could run free, and Slatey was on them.

Few modern hens are allowed to live longer than one year, and the life-span of most cockerels is no more than twelve weeks, but Slatey lived on our farm for a least five years. Every spring she was a model mother, invariably becoming broody early and rearing a brood of chicks. Every summer she reverted to her role as a slayer of mice, besides dominating all the other hens in her flock. Even now, more than forty years on, I can still see her. I doubt whether she ever made much profit for the farm, but what a character she was!

The shepherd and the psalm

October 1982

It was, I suppose, commendable that the team of clergy who have updated the metrical version of the 23rd Psalm for inclusion in the new hymn-book, *Hymns for Today's Church* – recently launched, in a flurry of controversy, at St Margaret's Church, Westminster – did not use a computer to assist their endeavours or they might have finished up with something far worse. After all, one thing that computers have so far failed to do is to write inspired poetry. Not that this re-jigged hymn shows much evidence of inspiration, but at least it keeps the concept of a shepherd, whereas it could easily have substituted a paternalistic commissar.

Doubtless because I was reared with sheep I have a warm spot in my heart for them, daft creatures though they may be, and I still like to see due regard paid to shepherds. When I first visited America I was disconcerted to find shepherds being referred to as 'sheep-herders'. Talk about retrogression! The English word started that way, a millenium ago. In the Anglo-Saxon rural economy a villager who herded sheep was, naturally, a 'sheep-herder'. Centuries of usage and an innate appreciation of harmonious language gradually softened it into the aesthetically satisfying word, 'shepherd'. Why go back to the gauche beginning?

My father started his working life as a shepherd boy. At the age of fourteen he first lambed down a flock of ewes on the hill overlooking our native village. At the age of 84 he lambed down a flock on the same hill. It seemed a kind thing for me to do, to buy a little flock of those delightfully docile sheep, Devon Closewools, to share his last years.

Now I treasure his crook, his bells and other paraphernalia of his craft. Appreciating that modern, urban, semi-pagan Britain cannot be expected to know much about sheep and shepherds, I sometimes think how fortunate I am to have been brought up with them.

The first lines of this new hymn are:

The Lord, my shepherd, rules my life
And gives me all I need.

Well, I suppose that accords with the sense of the Psalm, though 'The Lord is my shepherd; I shall not want' still seems better to me.

All through my farming years we usually had a flock of sheep on the farm. In January my father and I sat down and planned the cropping programme for their benefit. Already the lambing pen was being constructed against the side of a straw-rick on the sheltered side of a tall hedge at the foot of the downs. The ewes would lamb in February, and by the middle of March the young lambs would appreciate a bite of fresh, newly-sprouted grass. We made sure there would be a meadow waiting for them.

Later there would be a succession of other pastures, and then crops of vetches and turnips, the aftermath of the hay-fields and late summer sowings of rape or kale. Throughout the year, till all the lambs had departed and the time for mating came round again, not a week was left unprovided for.

What we planned for and worked for, the shepherd rationed out to the sheep. Every day his chief task was to pitch a hurdle fold enclosing tomorrow's allocation. While the sheep were eating he was preparing their rations for the next day. So it went on, all round the year.

I have no high regard for the mental powers of sheep and think it unlikely that they appreciated what was going on, but, supposing they could have known, the realisation would have come to them that, although they were doing nothing about it, someone they could trust was planning for them and someone was providing for their daily needs, and they were in a position to state with confidence, 'We shall not want.'

Other passages in the 23rd Psalm had special meaning for shepherds. In the next field to the sheepfold is a lush green pasture, luxuriant with grasses and clovers. The sheep gaze longingly at it, eager to charge in and begin the feast. But the shepherd drives them in the opposite direction, to a previously-grazed meadow where the grass is sparse and sere and brown. There all day long they have to work hard for their living, doubtless indulging in hard thoughts about their unfeeling shepherd. Then, when the sun is sinking low, they are allowed for an hour into the new pasture before they settle down for the night. The shepherd knows best. Fresh young grass and clovers give greedy sheep bloat. Gases accumulate in their stomachs, which distend painfully, and unless the shepherd arrives quickly to stick a canula into them they will die an agonising death. By working hard to fill themselves with dry grass all day they have made it safe to be allowed, in the evening, into the green pastures.

In a meadow near my home a farmer has a flock of Cheviot sheep, brought down from Scotland. Far from running away when a human approaches, they come towards him, for they have evidently been used to following a shepherd, rather than being driven.

It is good for sheep to behave like this, for by their nature they will follow somebody or something. In the South Country, where I spent my farming life, there was no tradition of training them to follow the shepherd, so they followed other sheep. Usually the leader of the flock was an old ewe who was versed in every ovine trick. She could be relied on to lead them in the paths of unrighteousness.

I once placed a flock of sheep on a 300 acre tract of downland, newly fenced and containing an abundance of grass. Before the first nightfall they were out on the highway. They had pushed their way through a cover of dense bushes to discover a small gap I had not noticed. I knew the old ewe who was to blame. I could appreciate what was in the poet's mind when he pointed out that sheep which followed the shepherd would not get into that sort of trouble; they would be led in the paths of righteousness.

I know, too, what the shepherd's rod and staff are. His staff is his crook, which enables him to catch and give medical care to any sheep which needs it. His rod is, or was, a short throwing-stick.

In the days when farm workers were not allowed to carry any weapon, for fear that they might use it on the landlord's game, a throwing-stick, apparently harmless, was permissable, though, in fact, most shepherds were deadly shots with it. Let a shepherd spy a rabbit or a pheasant crouched in a hedgerow and he did not lack meat for the pot next day. Ostensibly, however, the throwing-stick was a help in defending the sheep, against fierce dogs or snakes or anything else which threatened. The shepherd's rod and staff were a comfort to the sheep. It pleases me to have retained a specimen of both.

The shepherd had a little house next to the sheep-fold – a timber box on wheels, with a stove, a camp bed, and a box of medicines. The sheep knew it was there and knew that was where the shepherd lived. The last two verses of the Psalm suddenly change tense and refer to the future rather than the present. 'Surely' (just as surely as I follow the shepherd) 'goodness and mercy shall follow me; and I will dwell in the house of the Lord for ever.' Well, if not actually in the house, at least within sight of it.

Somehow I feel that if anyone rewrites the 23rd Psalm it ought to be a shepherd.

Here is the latest metrical version of the 23rd Psalm, an alternative to the one generally sung to the tune Crimond:

The lord, my shepherd, rules my life
and gives me all I need:
He leads me by refreshing streams
in pastures green I feed.
The Lord revives my failing strength,
He makes my joy complete,
and the right paths, for His name's sake
He guides my faltering feet.
Though in a valley dark as death,
no evil makes me fear;
your shepherd's staff protects my way,
for you are with me there.
While my enemies look on
you spread a royal feast;
you fill my cup, anoint my head
and treat me as your guest.
Your goodness and your gracious love
pursue me all my days:
your house, O Lord, shall be my home
your name, my endless praise.

A little heap of apples under the stairs

October 1986

'Where shall I put them?' enquired my wife, indicating a basket of apples a neighbour had given her. 'In the place designed for storing apples,' I told her, 'the bedroom window-sill.' Of course.

So now we fall asleep in a room fragrant with the scent of apples and pears, and when I wake up during the night I think for a moment that I am a boy again. For then my father not only had an orchard of his own but also purchased the fruit of other orchards, for sale on his retail round.

Every bedroom had heaps of apples on the floor, as well as those adorning the window-sill. At bedtime my brother and I had to pick our way between piles of Tom Putts, Beauty of Baths, Orange Pippins, Bramleys and the rest, all of which we could then identify by taste in the dark, though I am not sure that I could now.

'What about the little heap under the stairs?' put in my wife, willing to let me know that she remembered as much about these matters as I did.

Ah yes. The Wassailling Song:

Old Apple Tree! Old Apple Tree!
We wassail thee and hope that thou wilt bear
Hats full,
Caps full,
Dree bushel baskets full,
And a little heap under the stairs!

So we chanted on the eve of Old Twelfth Night when we went on to wassail the apple trees, anointing their roots with libations of cider, wedging cider-soaked toast in the branches for the robins to eat, and discharging shot-guns up through the branches to make sure the apple-tree goddess was awake and noting what we were doing. We wanted to ensure that no neglect of ours would deter the trees from bearing a good harvest next year.

And the cupboard under the stairs was certainly another recognised place for storing apples. Also sacks of gleaned wheat, in the days before we had a farm and my grandmother went gleaning.

Storage space was at a premium in cottage homes. Great-grandfather William has told me of an old chapel preacher who, living in a three-roomed hutch bursting at the seams like a long-tailed tit's nest with proliferating children, used to keep his family Bible, wrapped in oilskin, in a recess in the thatch over his back door. And storage space was what was needed in the autumn of the year.

It is axiomatic that farmers in Britain need to devote the five months of summer to growing and conserving crops to feed the farm livestock during the seven months of winter. Less generally recognised is the fact that, until well into the present century, the same forethought had to be applied to human needs. Cash being a scarce commodity in cottage homes, one didn't waste it on food that prudent parents could themselves provide.

In my boyhood home, a cottage enlarged to make a smallish farmhouse, an important feature of the kitchen was the bacon-rack. This was a series of planks, a foot or so apart, fastened to the great exposed beam in the ceiling. Autumn saw the sacrifice of the pig which had been fattening all the summer in the sty by the privy at the far end of the garden path.

I remember the ritual in which, on misty mornings in October or November, my father played the role of executioner, and in which I was a regular acolyte. The feast that followed, spread over a week or so, was one of the gastronomic highlights of the year.

Fresh meat was for once abundant, and we also tucked into such luxuries as chitterlings, faggots, scraps (crackling to northerners?), fried brains, melts, eye-pieces and other titbits which my mother understood well how to prepare. As this delectable period tapered off we were left with a store of hams, Bath chaps, brawn and sides of bacon. These last had been salted several times by having the salt well rubbed in, by hand, while they lay in a wooden silt. Sometimes one, or a part of one, was hung in the wide chimney, for smoking. When all the operations were finished, the cured bacon took its place in the bacon rack. As we sat at breakfast beneath it throughout the winter we could watch it gradually disappearing as my father, from time to time, cut off chunks of it, for slicing into rashers. Or often we simply had cold bacon for breakfast. Towards the end of winter the outside of the cuts tended to become rancid and had to be pared off, but that was regarded as evidence of imperfect curing.

The bacon rack in our house extended right to one wall, enabling the plank nearest the wall to be hung with strings of onions, bunches of herbs and basins of lard. The brawn, also in basins, shared a stonelined cupboard over the bread-oven with jars of pickles, sundry bottles of herbal remedies, several jars of slab-like vinegar plants and other mysteries. My mother baked an occasional batch of bread in the bread-oven, which, however, was used just as frequently for baking bags of feathers for stuffing pillows and cushions.

In our part of the country cheese was not often made, and we made butter every week throughout the year so did not need to store it (though we sometimes had to place the pats in cold water in warm weather). We did, however, sometimes smoke fish, in a home-made smoke-box, when my father brought home from market more fresh herrings than we could immediately eat. As I remember it, our smoke-box was a box or barrel let into the ground but equipped with ventilation and flues to ensure a steady current of air over the smouldering sawdust. I do recall that the sawdust had to be of oak.

Potatoes and all the root crops were stored in outdoor clamps, always known as pits, because at least half their area was below the surface. When in the late 1940s and 1950s I used to conduct quizzes on the radio or for Young Farmers Clubs one of the questions I sometimes asked was, 'What thatching job on the farm could you do without a ladder?' The answer was, 'Thatching a tatie-pit or a mangold pit.' I suppose the question would be meaningless now.

One of the gang

October 1987

Among the hundreds of thousands of children starting their school life in the autumn term which has just begun is a brave little four-year-old named Ian, who is attending a village school in Norfolk. Ian, who has cerebral palsy, can only walk with two sticks, but his parents have decided that the best chance of a normal life is in his village school, rather than a special one. Says his mother, 'Everyone knows him and he won't be a spectacle.'

How right she is.

Anyone who has lived for a time in Africa is bound to have been impressed by the African extended family. Every person belongs to a family, which includes uncles, aunts, cousins to the nth degree, grandparents and small sprouts of unknown paternity. Indeed, in many tribes a person can hardly be said to have a life outside his family. His family looks after him in every vicissitude, and he, for his part, is expected to look after his family.

True, this sometimes results in nepotism and what we would call corruption, as people in authority ensure that members of their family get the best jobs, and it is extremely hard to become rich because of the multitude of hangers-on that cluster around a successful man. When attempting to assess the need in a war area after a civil war in an African country I was amazed at the comparative emptiness of the orphanages. Nearly all the many orphans had been absorbed into extended families. 'We look after our own,' I was told.

The village of my boyhood days was not unlike that, and the similarity was even more pronounced in the time of my great-grandfather William. After all, most of the villagers were related. They were past the stage of 'having all things in common', but no-one went hungry, especially after harvest and at pig-killing time. We were reared in the knowledge that we 'belonged'.

The sense of a common identity, a sense of community, survives most strongly in the village school. In places today it is wearing a bit thin, due to the rapid changes in population. Those who through choice or necessity move house every few years lose their benefits of fitting in as integral parts of a social unit. But enough stay put to provide continuity and to keep the old tradition going. Evidently Ian, lucky chap, belongs to such a village.

Within such a community, physical or mental disability counts for very little. Last week, when my wife and I were keeping an eye on a young man who has a strange mental handicap, while his parents took a short holiday, I was discussing the background with a man who is of the same generation as my own children.

'Do you remember Jim?' he asked, and of course I did.

Jim would have struck an observer as being a pathetic case. His body and his face were twisted, his head lolled towards one side, and he constantly dribbled. His speech was slurred, his hands were warped, and he was confined to a wheelchair. To make matters worse, beneath all these handicaps he had a clear, normal mind. Life must have been terribly frustrating for him. But he went to the village school, and my friend was one of his classmates.

'Do you know?' he reminisced, 'we never noticed his disabilities. He was Jim, one of the gang. Where we went, he went. In his wheelchair. We must have pushed him for miles – over fields, through hedges, down hillsides with us hanging on grimly like human brakes! We helped him to keep score at cricket. We used his wheelchair, with him in it, to collect bushes for the bonfire on Bonfire Night.'

'We had to keep him away from the girls, though!' he added with a grin. 'Jim liked the girls!'

Most of the villages I knew when I was a boy had a resident like Jim. Someone not quite normal, either physically or mentally. Someone mentally retarded, or deaf-and-dumb, or with a cleft palate (which was then impossible to correct), or lame, or blind. All were accepted into their community. And, in the system of mixed farming then dominant, most were able to become absorbed in work on the land.

The young man who was temporarily under our care has teenage brothers and sisters. In fact, we were hardly necessary, for they took good care of him. His sister cooked and washed for him, made his bed and supervised his daily doses of pills. His brothers deliberately involved him when they were dismantling their motor-bikes and putting them together again. They evolved a rota which ensured that he would never be left alone in the house.

Perhaps even more remarkable to us, though they see nothing remarkable in it, is the fact that as the years pass and new boy friends and girl friends appear on the scene, they accept Frank too. They talk with him normally, buy him birthday presents. On Bank Holiday one brother and his girl friend took Frank with them to a vintage car rally.

When his parents returned from holiday, I congratulated them on the considerate behaviour the family showed towards Frank.

'It must have been difficult for them at times,' I suggested. They agreed. 'They have had to do a lot of adapting. But I think they're better for it.'

Lucky little Ian, to be able to look forward to a school life in an English village! And lucky, too, his classmates, for he isn't the only one who is going to be educated!

Solid pumpkins and ethereal ghosts

November 1987

Last weekend I harvested my giant pumpkin, which proved to be not so giant after all. It weighed 40 pounds, which is just 400 pounds short of the British record! Even so, my neighbours thought it quite impressive, but I know what I did wrong. I applied the sugar-water treatment too late.

The correct procedure is to place a jam-jar filled with a saturated solution of sugar against the pumpkin stem and allow a strand of wool, threaded through the stem, to dangle in the liquor. The pumpkin sucks up the sugar-water so rapidly that you need to renew the supply every day or so. The treatment should be started when the pumpkin is quite small, and I knew I had missed the boat when, on introducing the wool, I found the stem was so hard that I could hardly force the needle through it.

However, I was working on the right lines in other respects. The pumpkin was planted in a heap of well-rotted manure, and when promising fruit appeared I prevented any others from forming, so that it should have exclusive rights to all the plant food going. Incidentally, 440 pounds is the British record; *The Guinness Book of Records* states that a pumpkin weighing 612 pounds was grown in California in 1984, so quite possibly my forty-pounder will seem a midget to some readers in tropical countries.

And now, what to do with it? I must say that I am not very partial to the sweet pumpkin pie that Americans appreciate so much, but I like most savoury recipes. Serving them mashed with minced meat is perhaps the simplest way.

Some years ago I took the biggest pumpkin I have ever grown (a mere 95 pounds) to a harvest home supper and sold slices of it by auction afterwards. They sold quite well, and we were able to dispose of the lot. My forty-pounder is also going to grace a table at a harvest supper but I can guess at its destiny. Someone is sure to regard it as just the right size for a Hallowe'en lantern. Which gives it a dual-purpose, for the flesh removed during the hollowing-out process can, of course, be used for cooking.

In my boyhood recollections of Hallowe'en celebrations the hollowed-out lanterns we carried were not even turnip-lanterns but mangold. Most farms grew crops of mangolds for their cows, so there were plenty of big roots to choose from. Pumpkins were not widely known. They fell within the domain of the 'big house', the home of the squire who could afford to employ gardeners. Villagers grew marrows but seldom pumpkins.

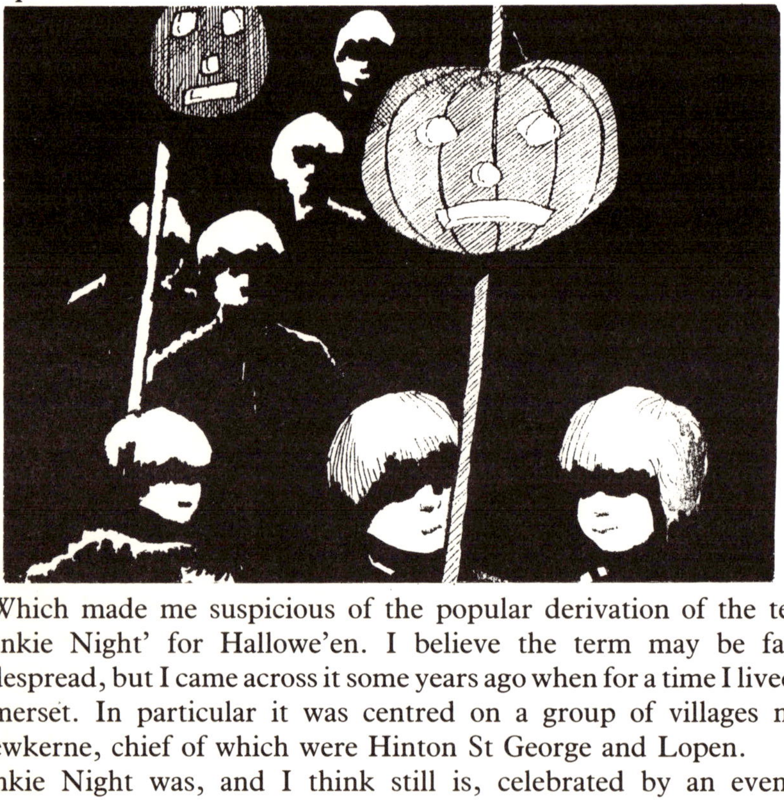

Which made me suspicious of the popular derivation of the term 'Punkie Night' for Hallowe'en. I believe the term may be fairly widespread, but I came across it some years ago when for a time I lived in Somerset. In particular it was centred on a group of villages near Crewkerne, chief of which were Hinton St George and Lopen.
Punkie Night was, and I think still is, celebrated by an evening procession, graced by a Punkie Queen and lighted on its way by innumerable lanterns carved out of pumpkins or turnips. Children in

fancy dress accompanied the decorated floats, chanting:

It's Punkie Night tonight,
It's Punkie Night tonight,
Gie us a candle, gie us a light;
For it's Punkie Night tonight.

There was even an improbable legend advanced as an explanation of the occasion. The women of Hinton, it was related, once became worried because their husbands were late home from Chiselborough Fair and feared that, under the circumstances, they were liable to fall off the single-plank bridge over a stream. So they called on their richer neighbours in order to collect money to buy candles to fit into pumpkin lanterns to light their errant menfolk home!

A likely tale! How long did all that take? one wonders. But local folk would countenance no criticism of it. How otherwise could Punkie Night have become associated with the pumpkin lanterns from which it took its name? Then another West Country-woman solved the puzzle for me.

'Punkie? Yes, of course. It's the will-o'-the-wisp!'

A punkie was a ghost associated chiefly with marshes. And Punkie Night being synonymous with Hallowe'en was a date when ghosts were liable to be around and when the autumn rains, following on the warmth of summer, tended to produce will-o'-the-wisps. They are, of course, wandering emanations of marsh gas, ignited by spontaneous combustion.

But I have never seen a will-o'-the-wisp, nor have I ever met anyone who has. In former times the phenomenon was much more frequent than it is now, presumably because there were far more undrained marshes. John Aubrey, the seventeenth century Wiltshire antiquary, once encountered a will-o'-the-wisp in a downland valley where one could never hope to see it now. And literature, which refers to it as Jack o' Lantern, Elfire, Ignis fatuus, Walking-fire, Star-spittle and half-a-dozen other imaginative terms, abounds in descriptions of it until well into the nineteenth century.

It would be interesting to hear from readers in countries still possessing undrained marshes whether they are familiar with 'punkies'.

Sounds of country music

December 1983

Recently, on November 12 to be precise, the Gothic arches of Salisbury Cathedral reverberated to the unaccustomed music of massed Salvation Army bands. The local churches and Salvationists from much of the south of England were celebrating the centenary of the founding of the first Salvation Army band, an event which occurred in Salisbury Market Place in 1883.

It happened in the most natural way possible. Most villages then had bands. My father was bandmaster of our village band, about fifteen musicians strong, in the years 1900 to 1910. He was a noted cornet-player, and one of the few photographs we have of my grandfather, about thirty years earlier, shows him, too, holding a cornet.

One of my father's treasured memories was of band practice under the great elm in the centre of the village on summer evenings. The lads and lasses, he remembered, would take off their footgear and dance barefooted on the grass. Happy days – at the threshold of this turbulent century and before the holocaust of the First World War.

Those of the bandsmen who were regular in church attendances naturally took their instruments to Sunday services. I myself remember that in the 1920s there were usually half-a-dozen cornet-players leading the singing at our village chapel. It was the custom. Sometimes, on fine summer evenings, they played hymns at a street corner for twenty minutes or so before marching to the chapel for the service.

The memories came flooding back one evening last summer when, to my surprise, I found a village band playing old familiar tunes on a village green in the New Forest. It was a strangely haunting and evocative experience.

At Alderbury, a village four miles from Salisbury, one of the leading cornet-players in the village chapel in the 1880s was Charles Fry. The holding of the first open-air meeting in Salisbury Market Place provoked considerable hostility and so became a general topic of conversation. Charles Fry determined to go and see what it was all about. Naturally, as the occasion was a religious service, he took his cornet with him, and naturally when the hymns were announced he accompanied them.

And that is how it all began. Old General William Booth, never one to miss a good thing, immediately saw the possibilities when he heard about the event, and bands were soon an integral feature of Salvation Army life.

Both the Army and its music were a product of the period in which they were born. Today's villages would have little in the matter of music to offer. A few village bands survive and do quite well in band contests, but the villages so blest are outnumbered by about twenty to one by those which are mute.

Not for many years have I attended a service in either church or chapel at which the musical accompaniment has been provided by anything other than organ or piano. Youngsters feeling an urge to produce their own music now seem to prefer the guitar. That, I suspect, is largely because you can form a guitar group with only three or four players, whereas for a brass or silver band you need a dozen or two.

I suppose the blame must be laid at the door of the instant availability of canned music. At the turn of a switch we can enjoy everything from pop to classical, whereas previous generations, if they wanted music, had to make their own. Parents of pop-addicted teenagers may well have had a surfeit of that type of music, more particularly because there is a tendency to measure its excellence by its volume.

Not so long ago, when fears had been expressed that working all day long with noisy tractors would damage the hearing of young drivers, I interviewed a young friend of mine to get his reactions. Climbing up a flight of steps to the cab of his giant vehicle, I enquired whether the continuous noise and vibration was driving him deaf.

'Eh?' he shouted.

I repeated the question.

'Wait a bit, while I switch this off,' he said. He had been listening, through ear-phones, to pop music going full blast.

It is true that work in the fields used to be a quieter occupation than it is now. You could plough all day to the muted accompaniment of the plodding of hooves, the occasional scraping of ploughshare against stone and the snorting of the horses. In the days when strong rivalry existed between farms as to which would get its harvest finished first, a triumphant team would raise a 'Harvest Shout' as they gathered the last

sheaf. It re-echoed across the fields and was sure to be heard by other teams still struggling with their corn. Nowadays it would be a waste of time, unless you waited for one of those brief lulls when no aeroplane was passing overhead.

The ubiquitous noises of modern life breed their natural and sometimes unfortunate reactions. Only the other day the papers carried the story of a group of suburban residents who got up a petition to stop the paper-boy and milk roundsman singing and whistling in the early morning.

Good heavens! It's ages since I heard any tradesman singing or whistling about his work. I myself hesitate to do so when out walking, for fear of popular disapproval. Or, more accurately, for fear that passers-by will think me mad. I had some queer looks when recently, I sat in my car at traffic lights, singing away merrily – forgetting that the side-screen had been wound down.

Even more unfortuate is the attitude to the sounds of the countryside. Periodically, though it seems quite regularly, we read in local papers of residents getting an injunction against one of their neighbours to make him prevent his cockerel from greeting the dawn with the traditional cacophany. One can appreciate that the reaction of a hundred pigs to a missed meal might be a little overpowering, but a cock crowing at dawn! - well, really!

Though, now I come to think about it, perhaps such an attitude is nothing new. I knew a keeper, living in a wood, who more than once threatened to take a shotgun to the nightingales which kept him awake at nights in June with their throbbing song, though I don't know whether he actually did so.

Making a beeline

October 1987

The two boys whom I was instructing in woodland lore solved to their satisfaction a problem which still has me puzzled.

'Why are these deer tracks always wiggly? Can't the deer walk straight?' asked Richard.

'Well, they've got to avoid the trees, haven't they, silly!' Mark retorted.

I let it go at that, though reflecting that in the adjacent fields I could have shown them deer tracks meandering just the same as among the trees.

Have you ever seen an animal track that is straight?

As a boy I used to have the task of taking the cows to pasture after the afternoon milking. I remember that to reach one luxuriant meadow we had to cross another large one obliquely, entering at one corner and striking across the middle to the distant opposite one. And I noticed that the cows, progressing crocodile-fashion, could never make a straight track. They kept swerving from side to side and then correcting themselves.

I dare say I remarked upon it because it illustrated a moral tale we heard more than once at Sunday School. A reward of sixpence was offered to which one of three boys could make the straightest track across a snow-covered field. One boy watched his feet. Another kept looking round to check on how he was doing. But the winner kept his eyes fixed on a mark on the far side of the field and went straight for it.

For animals in the wild there are too many distractions. Herbivorous animals such as cows cannot resist stepping aside to sample a luscious tuft of grass. Smaller mammals have to keep an all-round watch for predators; some of them, such as hares, have their eyes set in the sides of their head so that they can see both backwards and forwards. Predatory animals, though keeping their eyes fixed on their prey, instinctively take advantage of every bit of cover.

But that is not the whole story. Last winter when snow fell overnight on an ice-covered pond I inspected the tracks on it. While birds, chiefly pheasants, pottered about along the edges, two animals, a roe deer and a badger, struck across the middle. The deer's track wavered and meandered, just like its normal tracks in the woods; the badger's made a broad, sweeping curve, with squiggly bits at either end.

Nature abhors straight lines. The two proverbial metaphors for straightness are entirely incorrect. We speak of 'making a beeline', but have you ever watched a bee leaving its hive and setting out on its quest for honey? It moves in a series of great arcs. And we refer to the direct distance between two points as being 'as the crow flies'. Well, a crow's path through the air is more direct than a wandering country lane but is by no means straight.

Even humans, unless they make a conscious effort, do not walk straight. Those same country lanes have their origin in footpaths trodden by human feet.

But give to me an English lane
That twists and turns, and turns again,
And pauses to sit down and drowse
Amid the meadow with the cows.

The tendency to wobble, when you come to think of it, is puzzling. Why should it be more natural to meander than to go straight? Again watching the cows, I think I detect what may be the answer. As they plod heavily along, their lumbering great bodies seem to veer to the left. After a dozen paces or so they realise they are going off-course, so they correct the drift. But soon they have forgotten and are swerving leftwards again. Is this valid for other animals, too? If so, has it something to do with the spinning of the earth? Do animals in the southern hemisphere have a tendency to the right?

Certain fellow dowsers of mine have their own theory on the matter, derived from the late Guy Underwood, who maintained that a maze of 'force-lines' or 'aquastats' existed which can be detected by persons with dowsing ability. These invisible track-lines converge and form spirals around certain spots which he termed 'blind springs'.

Dowsers of this school assert that animals, birds and indeed all forms of life except ourselves, are aware of these blind springs, and that in us the power did exist until we allowed it to atrophy. Animals, they say, select blind springs as the proper places to give birth to their young. Birds build their nests over the spirals; insects are attracted by them. More relevant to the subject we are discussing, walking animals follow the invisible track-lines.

Well, I can dowse, to the extent of being able to locate underground water or drains or buried objects, but mapping out force-lines is too complex and intricate for me. Guy Underwood claimed to detect no fewer than seventeen blind springs under one stone, the so-called Slaughter Stone, at Stonehenge. But I have doubts about whether aquastats and force-lines can account for the course taken by animal tracks. The badger and the roe deer which marked those irregular tracks across my snow-covered pond last winter were walking over water.

When, as a boy I used to take the cows to pasture after milking there was one large field which could be approached from several directions. Well-marked, meandering cow-paths converged on a point somewhere near the centre. What was the attraction at that point? A blind-spring? No, a water-trough!

However, it is easier to criticise a flawed idea than to suggest a valid alternative.

Magic mummery at midwinter

December 1986

A few years ago, when I was a regular panel member in a television quiz programme, I offered for the mystification of my fellow members a performance of a Christmas Mumming Play.

I was not really surprised when they identified it almost immediately for Mumming Plays, after having become nearly extinct, have recently been enjoying a new vogue. Local groups of players have recognised their dramatic possibilities and have assiduously collected any memories of dialogue and action that have survived.

The plays are essentially associated with the winter solstice, presenting in dramatic form the battle between light and darkness. On December 21 the long retreat of the sun ends. The forces of light have fought the enemy to a standstill and from this day will start to drive him back, till spring and summer come again.

'It's magic,' as Paul Daniels would say, and so a key figure in the play is the Medicine Man, or Doctor, who by his magic physic restores the fallen hero to life. Undoubtedly the plays have their roots in primitive religion, and no priest worth his salt would miss the opportunity for claiming credit for the beneficent sequel.

Over the long centuries the plays were updated perhaps dozens of times. In the Middle Ages the champion of the light became identified with St George, the knightly patron saint of England. The natural adversary of knights at that period were the infidels they encountered when going on a Crusade, so he became known as The Turkish Knight. Until antiquarians started to collect them when they were almost obsolete, the words of the plays were never written down. They were passed on orally, and every player had to repeat exactly what he had heard, whether the words appeared to make sense or not. And so the line

'My carol is done' might appear in a version of the play as 'My curls are down', a combatant is described by the unknown adjective 'creagious', St George becomes 'King George'. and The Turkish Knight is found masquerading as 'The Turkey Snipe'. Sometimes preceded by a herald, St George enters, introduces himself, recounts some of the mighty deeds he has performed and engages in some robust boasting. He is interrupted by the arrival of The Turkish Knight, who accepts his challenge. They fight, and presently St George falls mortally wounded. A cry goes up for a doctor, and the medicine man hurries on, carrying a black bag of medicaments. He too boasts of all the impressive cures he has effected in remote parts of the world, extolling the properties of his magic Opliss Popliss Drops which, he says, will cure:

> *imples, pimples, simples, the itch, the stitch, the palsy and the gout;*
> *pain within and pains with out.*

He pours medicine down the throat of the stricken St George, who leaps to his feet, restored to complete vigour and starts a new fight with his dark adversary. This time, of course, he wins.

It sounds simple, rather childish stuff, yet its dramatic possibilities are impressive. The performance we recorded for television was staged on a refectory table occupying the centre of an old barn which had been transformed into a village inn. The spectators sat around at tables or around a blazing log fire, drinks at their elbows. The New Forest Mummers who gave the show were lively and energetic. St George and The Turkish Knight leapt on to the table without recourse to the steps provided and went at it hammer and tongs. The Doctor supplied light relief by nearly choking St George when he administered a draught of the magic elixir.

One could appreciate why the play survived for all those centuries; why it nearly died in the past hundred years was more of a puzzle.

The key is to be found in two other characters who have crept in. One is Little Johnny Jack. The archetype of the insignificant hen-pecked husband he is dressed in rags to which are pinned ten or a dozen scruffy dolls, representing children. His introductory speech runs something like this:

In come I, Little Johnny Jack,
With my wife and my children on my back.
Out of eleven I have but seven,
And three of them are gone to heaven.
One to the Workhouse he is gone,
And the rest will go when I get home,
And although I am but short and small,
I'm the biggest rogue among you all.

The other new character is Father Christmas, who acts as compere. His role is to introduce the characters as they appear, to call for the Doctor and to make the final speech, as follows:

Roast beef, plum pudding and mince pie,
Who likes them better than Johnny Jack and I?
Nobody!
A jug of Christmas Ale, sir, will make our voices ring.
Money in our pockets is a very good thing.
So, ladies and gentlemen, be at your ease,
And give us poor Mummers just what you please.

It is unashamedly a begging speech, and it reveals for whom the plays were performed. The Mummers were local peasants and labourers who had formed the custom of presenting them in the hall of the 'big house' at Christmas and asking for alms. It gave them a legitimate opportunity for seeking charity from the rich. They had a vested interest in keeping the tradition alive.

The reaction of the audience can be judged from the fact that the literature of the cultured and the fashionable in the eighteenth and early nineteenth centuries contains hardly any reference to the mumming plays. It seems that they were regarded with benevolent indifference.

So, when towards the end of the nineteenth century life gradually improved for the rural poor and economic ills beset the country landowner, the incentive to keep the plays alive was lost. In my native Wiltshire, nine villages were still performing them in the early 1930s but all had ceased by the end of that decade. Scripts have been prepared for some of them, from the memories of old men who once took part, but for many villages little remains except the memory that they once had mummers.

Curious incidental details attached to some of the plays suggest their very ancient origin. One is that the players in many instances were required to blacken their faces or to wear masks. That is in keeping with the venerable belief that a player in a sacred drama must at all costs be anonymous. He must be entirely submerged in the character he is portraying, beyond any possibility of being recognised by the spectators as someone they know in everyday life.

Another is the appearance, in the Midlands and in Dorset, of the character Beelzebub, a giant, in the place of Little Johnny Jack. His introductory speech is:

In comes I, Be-elzebub,
And on my shoulder I carry a club;
In my hand a frying-pan;
Don't you think I'm a jolly old man?

The frying-pan is used to take up the collection at the end of the play. Now the huge hill figure of the Cerne Abbas Giant, Dorset, carries in its hand a great club, while on the hilltop above its head is a prehistoric earthwork known as The Frying-pan. Significant?

Neglected treasure

December 1985

The girl sitting next to me fumbled for her handkerchief, dropped it and knocked her book on to the floor, with an embarrassing crash that the echoing church magnified. We nine readers were lined up in the front pew, waiting to participate in the service of Nine Lessons and Carols which has become a conventional part of Christmas in the 1980s.

'Oh dear!' she whispered. 'Now I've lost my place. Where do I look for it in this book?'

The Bible, of course. So I found it for her, marvelling that, even in the twilight of a church before the candles were lit, she could not turn unhesitatingly to the story of the shepherds in St Luke, chapter 2.

I suppose the custom was becoming anachronistic even then, but when I was a boy we engaged in family prayers every morning. My father came in to breakfast after feeding the pigs and calves, supplying them with fresh litter and helping with the milking. The real work of the day started after breakfast, but, with the early chores finished, there was no reason for undue haste over the meal. When everyone had finished eating my father pushed aside his plate in order to accommodate the big family Bible and read a selected passage. Then he knelt to deliver a short extemporary prayer, concluding with the Lord's Prayer. We had no telephone in those days but, had we possessed one, I am sure my father would have taken it off the hook before prayers began. So the day got off to a good start.

From contemporary literature one gathers that morning prayers and Bible reading were customary in the homes of both rich and poor for at least three centuries before the present. Admittedly standards of behaviour frequently did not match this pious custom, but beyond doubt it was an influence for good and our present society is the worse for having abandoned it.

For me, however, I think that much of its value lay in the introduction it gave me to good literature. If I have ever achieved anything worthwhile with my pen (meaning my typewriter!) it is to a great extent due to the magnificent work done by King James I's panel of scholars, who dealt in pure poetry.

'How beautiful upon the mountains are the feet of him that bringeth good tidings!'

To the pedantic scribe of the sort who churn out gobbledegook for government departments it is meaningless, yet it conveys exactly the mood for which the writer is striving.

'He shall be as an hiding place from the wind, and a covert from the tempest; as rivers of water in a dry place, as the shadow of a great rock in a weary land.'

Oh, I like Isaiah.

And have you ever heard, as I did on the Sunday after VE-Day in 1944, a public reading of chapter 14 of Isaiah? Try reading aloud verses 4 to 20, and imagine what a preacher with a good voice could make of that, when referring to the doom of Hitler.

Never use a long word when a short one will do just as well, was a rule I learned early at school. Do you know that in the familiar Psalm 23 only 20 of its 118 words have more than one syllable? And several of those are due to the now obsolete use of the suffix 'eth', instead of the 's' that we would employ.

Yet what of this passage, again from Isaiah? 'He that is so impoverished that he hath no oblation chooseth a tree that will not rot ....' If the writer had observed the rules he would have written, 'He that is so poor that he has no gift to bring.....' But the contrast between that first sonorous phrase and the simple language that follows is far more effective. It is a splendid example of how inspiration can ignore the rules.

The gems of the Bible are scattered in all manner of obscure places. For instance, where would you find this familiar quotation: 'For the earth shall be filled with the knowledge of the glory of the Lord as the waters cover the sea?' In the Book of the Prophet Habakkuk.

I was more than grateful for my knowledge of the Bible when, two years ago, my wife had to undergo a severe operation for a brain haemorrhage and was not expected to live. I knew just where to find a passage that began to run through my mind. 'Prove me now herewith, saith the Lord, if I will not open you the windows of heaven and pour you out a blessing there shall not be room enough to receive it.'

It seemed an impossible promise, but that is exactly how it has worked out for us. The quotation is from the Book of Malachi, and here are some more, not unfamiliar, from the same unfamiliar book.

'They shall be mine, saith the Lord, in the day when I make up jewels.' 'Unto you that fear my name shall the Sun of righteousness arise with healing in his wings.' (Analyse it, word by word, and it means nothing, but how could the thought be better expressed?) 'Behold, the Lord whom ye seek shall suddenly come to his temple.'

Consider, too, how penetrating are some of the expressions used. In the Parable of the Prodigal Son we have a picture of a wayward young man who made a predictable mess of his life and then, reduced to eating pigs' food, bitterly blamed everyone else for his plight. Until one day he could find no-one else to blame, and then 'came to himself'. And that was when he discovered someone who could do something to remedy matters.

I was reared in an atmosphere of church and chapel tea-meetings and was familiar with what went on behind the scenes, in the vestry and kitchen. So I knew what the Prophet Zechariah was on about when he wrote, 'In that day the pots in the Lord's house shall be like the bowls, before the altar.' The sparkling, polished bowls and the greasy pots. There never has been a more perfect affirmation of the equality of men in the sight of God.

After days of travelling over the burning, dusty plains of India, visiting innumerable temples and shrines to multifarious deities, I stood in the spacious coolness of the great Cathedral Church of Medak and read the inscription, from the Book of Revelation, in huge, towering letters above the altar:

I AM HE THAT LIVETH, AND WAS DEAD;
AND, LO, I AM ALIVE FOR EVERMORE AND HOLD
THE KEYS OF DEATH AND OF THE HEREAFTER.

As I move towards my twilight years I find myself reassured by that tremendous claim.

What a treasure we neglect when we use the Bible merely as a convenient stand for a flower-vase.